Meeting, Mating, and Cheating

Sex, Love, and the New World of Online Dating

Meeting, Mating, and Cheating

Sex, Love, and the New World of Online Dating

Andrea Orr

REUTERS

Library of Congress Cataloging-in-Publication data

Orr, Andrea

Meeting, mating, and cheating: sex, love, and the new world of online dating/Andrea Orr.
p. cm.
ISBN 0-13-141808-4
1. Dating (Social customs)--Computer network resources. 2. Personals--Computer
network resources. 3. Man-woman relationships--Computer network resources. 4. Mate
selection--Computer network resources. 5. Interpersonal relations--Computer network
resources. 6. Internet--Social aspects. I. Title. II.
Title. III. Series.

HQ801.O77 2004
306.7'0285--dc21   2003056539

Editorial/production supervision: *Nicholas Radhuber*
Cover design director: *Jerry Votta*
Cover design: *Design Source*
Interior design: *Gail Cocker-Bogusz*
Manufacturing manager: *Alexis Heydt-Long*
Executive editor: *Jim Boyd*
Editorial assistant: *Linda Ramagnano*
Marketing manager: *Laura Bulcher*

Reuters:
Executive editor: *Stephen Jukes*
Coordinating editor: *Giles Elgood*
Commercial manager: *Alisa Bowen*

© 2004 Reuters
Published by Pearson Education, Inc.
Publishing as Reuters Prentice Hall
Upper Saddle River, New Jersey 07458

Prentice Hall offers excellent discounts on this book when ordered in quantity for bulk purchases
or special sales. For more information, please contact:
U.S. Corporate and Government Sales
(800) 382-3419
corpsales@pearsontechgroup.com.

For sales outside of the U.S., please contact:
International Sales
1-317-581-3793
international@pearsontechgroup.com

Company and product names mentioned herein are the trademarks or registered
trademarks of their respective owners.

Printed in the United States of America

10 9 8 7 6 5 4 3 2 1

ISBN 0-13-141808-4

Pearson Education Ltd.
Pearson Education Australia Pty, Limited
Pearson Education Singapore, Pte. Ltd.
Pearson Education North Asia Ltd.
Pearson Education Canada, Ltd.
Pearson Educación de Mexico, S.A. de C.V.
Pearson Education—Japan
Pearson Education Malaysia, Pte. Ltd.

Contents

INTRODUCTION

I first became aware of the Internet dating trend back in 1999 when a guy I work with was dumped by his girlfriend. For a couple of weeks he moped around the office, but then, just like that, he was out of the doldrums and back in circulation. Several mornings each week, he'd arrive at work and regale me with some story of an adventure with a new woman he'd met the night before: the eccentric woman, the tall woman, the woman who had just returned from a trip around the world who couldn't stop talking about Nepal. All had come into his life through a personal ad he'd placed online, and he was a very busy man. Even at the office, when he wasn't working at his job, he seemed to be consumed with a second job of maintaining his social life: firing off thoughtful emails to the women he'd seen the past couple of nights, responding to those who had seen his ad, cruising through the list of new personals for that elusive, perfect match. There were always more to choose from.

I'd been dumped by my boyfriend around the same time, but I took more of a passive let-life-come-to-you approach to personal matters. I continued to mope long after my colleague had moved on. He'd type away at the email, periodically laugh uproariously, or naughtily, at a response he received, and then leave promptly at five o'clock for another night on the town. At the desk beside him, I watched with curiosity, and probably a little jealousy. It seemed he had found a shortcut through the dry spells, a kind of high-tech way around the old limits of available people you could meet in the normal course of your life.

I should have spotted a trend back then. Although Internet dating was not nearly as big as it would become, it was already being used by thousands of people. And I was working as a reporter in Silicon Valley at a time that would come to be known as the dot-com boom. The whole point of my job was to write about promising new Internet technologies. I wrote all about the Internet bookstores and Internet furniture stores, and many more obscure things too, such as online bridal registries, and specialized Web sites that sold nothing but ink for your printer, or tube socks. But I failed for a long time to see Internet dating for the phenomenon it would become: one of the most lucrative dot-com business models that would transform the community it served.

Instead, I saw newspaper personal ads transferred online. Newspaper personals had been around for decades. Old service. New format. What was the news in that? Besides, while my colleague was definitely getting a social workout, I could not see what it all amounted to. As he eased out of rebound mode and began searching for something more substantial, he seemed to tire of the easy access to women with whom he may or may not have had anything in common. One especially memorable evening, we spent hours in a bar as he tried to mentally prepare himself for a formal dinner date with a woman he had met the week before. She was cute, she was nice and she was single. Ready, willing and able, so to speak, and according to that optimistic yet slightly fear-inspiring "don't miss out" tone that so many dating companies took, he ought to be jumping at the opportunity to see her again. But he felt nothing. As we finished our second martinis and he debated whether it would be wise to have a third before dinner, I started to think that it wasn't so wrong to let life come to you.

Still, this colleague of mine was a perfectly pleasant, nice-looking, intelligent and normal guy who had a great personality and no glaring social flaws that would have stopped him from meeting someone in the traditional way. I had never known anyone like him to post a personal ad in the back of a newspaper, at least not with such a lack of hesitation or apology. Not only was he using these online personals—something I had just assumed to be the realm of the sleazy or the slightly desperate—but he was openly talking about it. So was a woman down the hall, I learned, when she finally told me why she was always coming into my office with a camera and asking me to take close head shots. From her, I discovered that the guy upstairs was on the Internet too. She knew, because the online dating service she had joined kept sending his picture to her, unsolicited, as one of the eligible singles nearby. Little did they know just how nearby he was.

But it was not just that so many young and attractive people were doing this and often doing it openly. The whole way in which they proceeded seemed different than the way I understood newspaper personals to work. These online daters would sign up and boom, just like that, have what seemed like hundreds of people to choose from. Often they would meet one right after the other, becoming so distracted by the wealth of options that they seemed free of that sense of lonesome longing that is associated with singles events. Even if they found no one who came close to resembling a soul mate, they were meeting people who were nice more often than they were creepy. And a good number of them were finding more than just a friend. Just within my extended circle of acquaintances, I could soon count several marriages that had grown out of online introductions.

There was something else, too, that I discovered after my colleague finally showed me the ad he had written. No typical single white male was he. His ad was nuanced, funny and self-deprecating, poking fun at his height, and even his insecurities, which he explained had all been caused by one defining moment during his childhood when his mother had sent him off to school with a Wonder Woman lunchbox. He wrote that his first name translated to mean "tall dark warrior" and that he supposed his parents had chosen that name to show that they had a sense of humor. That little 400-word piece of prose was witty and intelligent. Was it a stretch to call it literary? If I had thought about it then, I would have realized that online personals were not just newspaper personals transferred online. They were a whole new genre, and they were fun. Some of the dating companies themselves did not know just how entertaining their services had become, but the entertainment value has proven over time to be a factor in attracting people to online dating and getting them to renew their subscriptions, often just for the fun of it. Today, several years after the dot-com craze ended, online dating has proven the exception to the rule: one of the few Internet business models that have endured.

When I began my research in earnest, I found a story that was far more complex than I'd imagined. Internet dating had done more than just make a small fortune for some companies and gotten a lot of single people off their couches. It had started to change the way people socialized in some pretty profound ways. Many singles were conducting prolonged correspondences over email before they ever met. And some of these people said they had become so addicted to the format, and the embellishment it encouraged, that it had become a social crutch. They were more fearful than ever of face-to-face contact. Then there were the restless married people, who often had the opposite response. For them, the Internet had provided a quick, safe and almost foolproof way to have an affair. One man even posted an advertisement stating the route he took on his commute home and the time he left work each night, saying he would love to connect with a woman who lived on the way, any time between 6:30 and 7:30. Infidelity was not new, but surely it had never been this easy.

There were more subtle things too. A phenomenon of hyper-dating that sometimes meant multiple dates with different people in a single week, and other times meant searching on your cell phone for someone near the coffee shop you were in, and hooking up five minutes later for coffee, or something else. This was starting to upset traditional notions of courtship, not to mention playing hard-to-get. I talked to healthy single men who said the Internet had killed their sex drive by providing such an abundance of willing partners and virtually no challenges. And I spoke to women who said they didn't believe that all the men they met online were weird, but they did think that the anonymity and fast pace of the Internet had led good men to behave badly. Men and women alike said they wondered if it was good to have a format where you could list your desires so specifically, and then eliminate anyone who did not match up. The guy who was perfect in every way, except that he was 5'8" tall, could find himself out of the running just because his ideal mate had listed 5'9" as her cutoff height.

And for all the happily married couples who said they never would have found each other had it not been for the Internet, I found many, many other singles who had been trying it for years with no success. Internet dating is often seen in two distinct ways: by the people who are successful, as a way to find your soul mate; or, by the cynics, as a magnet for undesirables. The reality I found was far richer: an array of good, bad, ugly, but mostly just very interesting stories. Stories of the seniors who found romance again for the first time in 50 years. Of women in Iran who went online to test the limits of their country's social constraints. Isolated small-town people used the Internet to find mates in other countries. Bartenders used it because they were tired of the bar scene. There were all sorts of stories, and many of them were pretty entertaining.

My favorite online dating story is one of stunning coincidence, and it comes from the very same colleague who first turned me on to this whole topic. Three years after he became a dating machine with the help of the Internet, he found true love online. And he found it with someone very close to home, an old classmate from grade school, who had either never noticed the Wonder Woman lunch box or had forgiven the infraction. As they toasted each other at their wedding one chilly January evening, they recited the ads that they had written a couple of years before, and they did so with pride. Geography had brought them together as school kids, and it seemed it was fate that had brought them together again years later. Fate, and the Internet.

ACKNOWLEDGEMENTS

I have many people to thank for helping me write this book and that list needs to begin with all the people, mentioned by real name or pseudonym, who shared some very personal stories. Special thanks to Angelo DiMeglio and Julie Fitzpatrick, who for month after month filled me in on all the ups and downs of their love lives. They helped put a real face on what is too often an anonymous story of looking for love online, and gave this book color and depth.

My editors at Reuters, especially Kevin Krolicki, Arthur Spiegelman, Adam Tanner, Janie Gabbett and Stephen Jukes, were extremely generous in giving me time off to write this book; and many of my overworked colleagues took on an extra workload in my absence. Peter Millership and Giles Elgood offered careful editing and patiently kept track of all my last-minute revisions. Alisa Bowen at Reuters and Jim Boyd at Prentice Hall kept the project on track every step of the way from the initial concept through to the cover design.

Many friends came through in many ways from help with research, last-minute editing and proofreading, hospitality, cheap travel arrangements, and moral support. They include Elinor Mills Abreu, David Brinkerhoff, Anne D'innocenzio, Kim Girard, Paul Lanyi, Lama Mansour, Tony Munroe, Rick Nash, Neil Robinson, Doug Young and Sue Zeidler. Lisa Baertlein was very helpful with research and also bore the brunt of the extra workload at Reuters while I was away. Carolyn Brown was the one who initially encouraged me to write a book on this topic. Sohail Kaleem served as my own personal help desk and helped make the technological challenges of working from a home office a little less daunting. Megan Adams, Elyse Klein and Sally Schillaci were especially helpful with research in the U.S. Jim Shissler was especially helpful with research in Asia.

My sisters MaryAnn Nash and Amanda Orr were a huge source of encouragement and support, as was my mother, Patricia Orr. She went beyond the call of duty, and proved extremely helpful with research, steering me toward a number of real life online dating stories, which made this a much richer story than it would have been without her contribution.

Author's Note

When I set out to write a book about how online dating had gone mainstream, I quickly discovered the real story was not so simple. In truth, attitudes are still all over the map and for every person who openly admits to using an Internet dating service, there are others who still log on in secrecy. Some married people boast about having met online, but others find it a source of embarrassment and go to great lengths to concoct stories of how they met offline at a party or through friends.

While I interviewed many people who had no problem seeing their real names in print, others were happy to share their stories, as long as they remained anonymous. As a result, I have had to use a combination of real names and pseudonyms. Whenever possible, I used people's real identities, and their first and last names. For those people who did not wish to be identified, I used a fictitious first name, no last name, and changed some other superficial details, such as their profession or city of residence. The easiest way to tell the difference is that anyone identified by first name only has used a fictitious name.

1

SEX, COMPANIONSHIP AND POWER TOOLS

"I am not very interesting on paper, but email me to get to know the real me."

—Online ad from a 23-year-old Minnesota man

When it came to her ideal man, Annabel[1] had a list. Not a very long list, and she didn't think it was all that demanding. But he was nowhere to be found.

"I want the package," the 40-year-old divorced mother would reply when people asked her why she didn't get out more. "I'm used to having it all: the sex, the companionship, and the handy guy around the house. If I can't have it all, it's sort of like, why bother?"

But Annabel was lonely. She had moved from suburban Washington, D.C., after her divorce to be closer to her family, to a town

---

1. Names and identifying personal details of all people mentioned by first name only have been changed to protect the individuals' privacy.

of 5,000 people in northern New England, where she had been unable to find a sexual partner, a male companion or a handy man—let alone all three in one. A natural beauty who had always managed to turn heads, Annabel had spent the first year after her divorce assuming that when she was ready, another man would somehow appear in her life. Four years later, as she faced another holiday season on her own, her frustration was becoming overwhelming. Often, it was the little things. There were a lot of little things, like the blown fluorescent lighting tube over her kitchen table that, for lack of anyone to fix it, had remained unchanged for weeks, forcing Annabel and her three young children to eat dinner each night by candlelight. There were bigger things, too, like the long, empty expanse of time that awaited her every night after the kids went to bed. One evening, she caught herself sorting their Halloween candy into separate piles of chocolates, suckers, gum and chewy stuff. "Too much free time," she confessed.

When it came to socializing during normal hours though, Annabel did not have much time at all. Hers was a typical story. Being a single mother to three young children, juggling part-time work, part-time schooling, an 80-mile round-trip commute and a battle to recover $20,000 in back child support, when was she supposed to get out? Where was she supposed to go? Annabel really did not have a clue about how to look for a man, even if she had had the time. She had married her high school sweetheart, and from age 17 on had never had to think about finding a date. She was a stranger to bars, email, or Stairmaster flirtations and all the other things perennial singles do, like sign up for Italian class just to meet some new faces. Still, she was not ready to put herself into social retirement. For all the ten years of marriage she had behind her, the painful discovery that her first and only love had been unfaithful, and the challenges she faced raising a family alone, Annabel did not look like a harried mom. She looked closer to 30 than 40 with a trim figure and a relaxed smile that showed no trace of the ordeals she had been through. She could not believe there was nobody out there for her, so she tried to focus on the ways new men might appear. It would be a new semester in a few months, she thought hopefully. Perhaps that would bring a new teacher or two to the school where she taught. Maybe one of those new teachers would be a man, and maybe he would be single. And maybe, just maybe, she would like this man, the one and only eligible bachelor to appear in her life in more than a year. She could always hope, even if the odds seemed impossible.

Overnight, those odds improved dramatically after Annabel took a friend's advice and signed up for an Internet dating service. It was the end of 2002, and all sorts of people who never dreamed they would do something so impersonal, so embarrassing or so desperate as post a lonely hearts ad in cyberspace were taking the plunge. Women's magazines that had once advised women on how to flirt in the grocery store began publishing articles about how to beguile over email; their tone wasn't so much advocating a revolutionary new social behavior as weighing in on what had become the status quo. The authors of *The Rules*, a popular 1996 book that urges women on the prowl to go back to old-fashioned, play-hard-to-get tactics, wrote a new book in 2002 about the rules of Internet dating, somewhat predictably advising women not to initiate email correspondence and to avoid all contact on Saturday night, even if they were home alone with nothing to do but log on. Although many people had already met online long before 2002, and thousands of them were married with children, interest in Internet dating suddenly exploded. Newspaper wedding announcements proudly proclaimed that the happy couple had met online. Wedding parties sometimes sported T-shirts or baseball caps bearing the logos of the dating service through which they had met, or even staged sentimental readings of the couple's personal ads, thumbing their noses at the notion there was anything to hide. As the year drew to a close, *The Wall Street Journal* placed Internet dating, along with Spanish red wine and Lucite bathtubs, on its list of what was in for 2003, and some experts predicted it would one day seem quaint that people had ever agreed to date without first screening their partner's bio online. Some insisted it was only a fad, but many others argued that Internet dating was no different than pay-at-the-pump gasoline or automatic teller machines: bound to be widely adopted because of the convenience it offered. It used to be said that you weren't going to meet anyone by staying in on a Saturday night, but now you could.

Annabel didn't know any of this when she signed up. In fact, she knew next to nothing about technology and did not even have Internet access at home. She also had a highly suspicious nature. "I wasn't exactly offended by the suggestion that I try it, but I didn't see myself doing it, either," she recalled later. "I guess I figured the guys would either be losers or criminals—those two categories, but not anyone normal. You figure a normal person could get a date without going on the Internet."

As soon as she started talking about normal people being able to find a date without any problem, she knew she wasn't making sense. Annabel had been on only four dates in two years, and those men had not even come close to meeting her list. So she agreed to check out some Internet personals sites, and when she did, her skepticism quickly softened. Scrolling through the photos of eligible men, she was soon taken with a photo of a guy her age, from a neighboring town, who had posed in front of his bicycle. The image was a bit grainy and shot from a distance, but Annabel liked it all the same. How about that, she thought, she liked to bike too. The sense of possibility was appealing, and much more promising than anything she had found at work or while waiting to pick up her daughter from gymnastics. With a little technical assistance from a friend, Annabel registered on the site and wrote up a brief profile describing herself as an avid cyclist who had liked to travel a lot, BC. Before Children, that was. Her description of her ideal man was incredibly blunt and honest. "Looking for the package," she wrote. "Sex, companionship and someone who can do the handy work around the house." And just like that, Annabel's barren dating world was suddenly overflowing with prospects. Her email box was overflowing, too. In a week she had more than 100 messages from suitors, including a local mail carrier and the fire chief of a nearby city.

The first person she heard from provided his own personal Q&A. (Q. What do you do for a living? A. Software Engineer. Q. If I could chose a superpower, what would it be? A. Ability to speak every known language, including talking to animals.)

Another sent a laundry list: "I'm 42, I tan easily, All of my teeth, ears, fingers, toes, etc. are intact, I like to read, I've been told I'm a great kisser, I own my own house."

One fancied himself a poet. "I can drill and paint, and promise not to make ya faint. I may be a sinner but would love to invite ya to dinner, if I don't hit my thumb first."

Some of these men were a little too warm, signing off their very first notes "thinking of you." Others too cold. "You sound good to me," one wrote. "I am ready when you are."

Some revealed almost nothing. Others, like The Rock, revealed a little too much.

"My friends and family describe me as their rock," wrote The Rock. "This is because I am a man of strong values...and because I am honest, loyal, sensitive and compassionate with unapproachable integrity. I am always there to help and support family and friends. Thus the nickname 'The Rock.'"

As she continued reading, Annabel felt herself getting closer.

"You sound like the perfect mate," wrote one man, who, like many others, said he liked quiet romantic evenings nestled by a fire sipping wine. "I believe I meet or even exceed your desires of having the full package. I am very handy and still have the sex drive of a 19-year-old, even though I'm 43."

The only problem, this suitor went on to say, was that he lived more than 100 miles away in a different state. The cute biker she had first noticed looked more problematic at second glance, too. In the few days it had taken Annabel to sign up and find her way around the service, he had taken down the picture of himself by his bicycle and posted another one, in which he was dressed up as a clown, face paint and all. "It was a turnoff," she complained. Plenty of others she was able to quickly eliminate as well, either on the basis of their photos or what they said. "One told me he had just moved his mother into his house with him, and I hit the delete button on that one in a hurry," said Annabel, who was still clashing bitterly with her former mother-in-law. She also found reason to be suspicious of people's claims. One day she came across a photo of a close coworker she knew to be married with two young children. He had joined the dating site, listing himself as divorced. Annabel started to wonder if it was all too good to be true. Maybe all these men were really married, maybe their photos were decades out of date. And she wondered if she would ever be able to take the next big step and actually meet one of these strangers. Online dating had not brought an end to her loneliness after all.

But it had piqued her interest. She wanted a man in her life and was willing to weed through all the cheaters and clowns to find one. The more she read through her email, the more she came across men who at the very least sounded like nice guys. Many commiserated that they too found computer dating a little awkward. A few had, like Annabel, spent time in California and were longing for its mild weather as the New England autumn found them scraping ice off their cars each morning. Lots were single dads who were devoted to their children. Most had a sense of humor. "I never imagined I would come across some woman's description of her ideal match and that description would describe me so perfectly," one wrote. "I do sex, companionship and power tools."

If nothing else, this was amusing. For the first time since her divorce, Annabel began looking forward to the weekends when her ex had the children so she could go to her sister's house and do email. After a few weeks of borrowing her sister's computer or stealing time at the library before the kids came home from school, she began looking around for the cheapest home Internet connection. Round-the-clock news, the convenience of online shopping or even a desire to be a part of the biggest media revolution of the late 20th century had not made her curious about the Internet, but online dating made her want to get connected.

While Annabel had been going through an ugly divorce, James Hong was living a carefree single life, working toward an MBA at the University of California at Berkeley, and worrying mainly about how he would make his first million. A product of the Internet boom of the late 1990s that had turned just about every other business-school graduate into a dot-com entrepreneur, Hong had technology in his blood. He passionately believed that the Internet was changing the world, and that a lot of people would make a lot of money in the process. You would not necessarily know it from his boyish looks, his mild manner and his self-deprecating humor, but Hong was driven. He so wanted to be a part of the high-tech revolution that after graduating he joined a networking group called Round Zero. The group brought together similarly ambitious people to debate the finer points of the new economy and swap business cards. In Hong's circle, people could entertain themselves for hours talking about the most inane business concepts, such as a project to build a Web site for expectant dads who were also sports fans, which would let them schedule a baby's birth so as not to interfere with the Super Bowl. Cocktail receptions were held to discuss Internet branding and whether a company's image was more important than its product. Some of the smartest minds in the business made a serious case for a new kind of Internet store where you would give the merchandise away for nothing and make up the difference by selling advertising.

Even the name Round Zero was an insider's reference, alluding to the three rounds of funding high-tech startups typically got before trying to raise money through the sale of stock. To be there at "round zero" was to be a true visionary who was present at the very time the business idea was born. That was how James Hong liked to see himself.

For all his devotion to the Internet revolution, though, Hong was no more clued in to the potential of online matchmaking than Annabel. Things like checking out women and making introductions over the Internet he saw as good fun, but not really a good business. After he finished business school and deliberated where he could get his best returns, he took a job with an Internet site linking businesses with other businesses, one of the so-called B2B sites that at the time were regarded as the next big thing in technology. The company Hong worked for linked various components of the construction industry, and there, he dutifully put in long hours trying to transform one of the most equipment-intensive industries into a nimble, virtual kind of Internet business. It didn't work. The company eventually folded. One night at a party, however, he and his roommate, Jim Young, both 27 at the time, were having more conventional fun trying to meet girls. When a friend remarked that one girl was a perfect 10, the group started talking about rating different women. And because this was a crowd of ambitious individuals who were a little obsessed with the Internet, it was natural that the conversation turned to an online rating system. They conceived of a Web site where people could post their photos for visitors to rate on a scale of 1 to 10. Never in a million years did they see such a Web site as the business that would make them rich. It was just a joke. Hong could only laugh when he kicked off this pet project by posting his own photo and received a lowly 3.8 out of 10 from his friends who visited the site.

As for the site itself, it quickly won perfect 10 scores all around. After getting some positive feedback from friends, Hong forwarded it to an investor he knew from Round Zero who liked it so much that he sent it to an online magazine journalist, who thought it was funny enough to write about. By the end of the week, AmIHotOr-

HotOrNot co-founders James Hong and Jim Young show off their less-than-perfect 10 physiques in a tongue-in-cheek ad for their Web site. Courtesy of Eight Days, Inc. Photography: Jock McDonald.

Not.com, an idea Hong admits was born with the help of a lot of alcohol, was being written about in *The Observer*, a British Sunday newspaper. "We launched it on Monday, and that Sunday it was in the London *Observer*," said Hong.

Did they ever see the site that is today called HotOrNot.com as a serious business? "No, no, no, no, God no," Hong said a few years later. It was not until other business ventures failed and HotOrNot took off that he and his partner began looking at ways to make money from the site. They added a function where visitors, after rating the photo, could attempt to connect with the person in the picture. And when membership became so big that they had to add computer servers to keep the site running, they added a modest $6 monthly fee for this so-called "meeting service." The fee was imposed only on visitors who wanted to write to other members, and then, only once they had secured an expression of interest from the person with whom they wanted to correspond. The idea was to charge as little as they could and still break even. Could they have charged more? "We probably could have," said Hong. "But I guess, being just two guys running it out of the house, we didn't feel like we needed to. Maybe we're bad business people."

Two years later, many of the other business plans hatched by fellow business school graduates and Round Zero networkers had failed, but HotOrNot was supporting its two founders in style. The site had millions of visitors and tens of thousands of paying customers, a number Hong and his partner Young hesitated to pin down since it would give away their own net worth. But they were not struggling. With the site requiring less than ten hours of their attention a week, Hong had plenty of time to explore other entrepreneurial projects, while Young, still a graduate student, could take his time finishing his Ph.D. in electrical engineering. And while other M.B.A.s who had arrived in Silicon Valley during the dot-com heyday were leaving town, or selling expensive cars acquired in better days, Hong defied the times. He upgraded from a Camry to a Porsche and chronicled the purchase in a tongue-in-cheek entry on his personal Web site as going from "not to hot."

Although HotOrNot is often regarded as an entertainment site catering to the most juvenile form of humor, it has produced several solidly happy couples. Bobie Covell was an 18-year-old waitress and aspiring singer from Farmington, Michigan, when her friend told her about the Web site as a place where you could "rate people if you are bored." Immediately, she heard from several guys, but Michael Karr's photo stood out, she said, because he was not only handsome, but also shared her passion for music. After emailing each other for four months, they exchanged phone numbers and embarked on another few months of daily phone calls that frequently lasted six hours. They discovered they had many other things in common. "He told me that he sometimes drives by people's garbage and picks things out," Covell said. "Me and my mom had recently found this nice entertainment center in other people's garbage. That was the first time we laughed together." Covell had heard stories about the reality not living up to the email personality and, fearing disappointment, put off meeting Karr. Her mother urged her to follow through. Six months after their first offline meeting, they were engaged, living together and sharing warm laughs about all of their strange shared interests like trash picking. Their story is not unusual.

Hong has a collection of fan letters from people all over the country who say they never would have found their soul mates had it not been for HotOrNot. What about any hate mail? No one was more surprised about the lack of that than Hong and Young themselves, who initially had kept their identities anonymous because they were so afraid people would be critical of the concept. They discovered that most people did not take the site that seriously, at least until they found a marriage prospect on it. And the way the audience naturally developed helped protect HotOrNot from the logical criticism that it was a site that objectified women. Currently, about 65 percent of the photos on the site are photos of men.

Hong didn't know it at first, but a whole new industry was being born around the notion that you could make money from matchmaking if you could just free people from the idea that love was supposed to be private, or spontaneous or all about the right timing. In 2002, Match.com, the biggest online dating service, saw its overall membership reach eight million, and its number of paid subscribers almost doubled from the year before to top 724,000. That same year, Yahoo Inc., the Internet media conglomerate offering all kinds of online services, began highlighting online personals more and more in its corporate presentations and talked about how that division had helped revive the entire company. Plenty of smaller sites catering to Christians, seniors, students, gays or other groups gained traction too. Marketdata Enterprises, a Tampa, Florida, group that tracks the matchmaking industry, estimated the online dating industry to be a $304 million business in 2002 as many players doubled revenues from the year before. By some estimates, 25 percent of single people in the United States were using online dating services by the end of 2002.

Normal people, like Matthew Bergstrom, a 30-year-old investment banker who frequently moved around between Europe, Washington, D.C., and San Francisco, and had met a series of women offline he did not consider his intellectual equals. Bergstrom liked how he could spell it out online, so he posted a profile saying he wanted to find "a terrific woman—cultured, beautiful, intelligent, adventuresome, book lover, good dancer, and much more." Just to drive the point home, he added "Turn-offs in the past have included 'Who is Winston Churchill?'"

John, a 35-year-old gay man living in New York City, said the Internet was a natural fit for homosexuals who often felt they lived outside of the social mainstream. "When you are a straight person, you meet people everywhere you go," he said. "Being gay, you've already eliminated 90 percent of the population." Henry, a 40-year-old marketing executive from Denver, said he just liked the efficiency of meeting people online.

All good points, but why the sudden explosion in Internet dating years after the appearance of online chat rooms and decades after newspaper personals ads began offering an alternative, but never entirely socially acceptable, way to find love? Melanie Angermann, who oversees marketing for Match.com, suggested that the online dating business was experiencing delayed adoption and the rapid growth rate companies typically see much earlier in their history. Traditionally, the earliest adopters of a popular new product became the evangelists and sent its growth on a sharp upward curve. But because people often were embarrassed to admit that they had placed a personal ad or gone to a matchmaker, the industry for a long time enjoyed almost no benefit of word-of-mouth referrals and moved along at a painfully slow growth rate, taking that much longer to reach critical mass.

Merri, a 33-year-old New York City journalist who met her husband on Match.com, is one of many satisfied customers who lied for a long time, making up stories about a chance meeting with her future husband at the gym, a friend's party or a bar. "It was embarrassing for me to admit," she said. "You tell somebody you met your boyfriend online and you watch their eyes very carefully, and a lot of times their eyes show shock and horror. They are like, 'Oh my God, you must be so desperate.' There's still a stigma of shame around it." Her friends may have been a little scornful at first, but when Merri became engaged, on the anniversary of her first email exchange, most of them started signing up. "One by one, they started dropping like flies," Merri laughed. Many more committed relationships followed. The same summer Merri got married, she and her husband attended six weddings, three of which had grown out of relationships commenced online.

"This category is so weird, it doesn't have any precedent," said Match.com's Angermann, citing the possible exception of plastic surgery, another consumer business that provides obvious benefits, but does not always receive customer testimonials. Internet dating might also be compared to getting a hair transplant or a breast augmentation for the way it has gradually become more acceptable, but is still not something everyone confesses to openly. The biggest dating sites today claim to have sitcom stars and national news anchors among their members, but say those famous clients do not want their names revealed. Many smaller celebrities, however, have provided endorsements. Amy Fisher, who as a teenager became the notorious Long Island Lolita and served seven years in prison for shooting her lover's wife, recently revealed that she met her fiancé through an Internet dating site. Vecepia Towery, who enjoyed her 15 minutes of fame as the winner of a Survivor competition, found her husband on Yahoo Personals.

And testimonials from average Joe types are cropping up everywhere. Recently, a Yahoo employee went to a friend's wedding and came back with an unusual party favor: a large block of chocolate wrapped in photocopies of the couple's first email exchanges, which it just so happened, had been initiated on Yahoo Personals. The wrapping paper traced the couple's courtship, starting with the first ad placed by Meg, a 47-year-old divorced mother who described herself as slightly overweight and "brimming with joy." The final message was the note Meg had received from her future husband right after their first date. "I feel like we are kindred spirits, and yes, I'm very interested in getting closer," he wrote. "I immediately canceled my pending ad on Yahoo. I think I have found what I was looking for."

2

THE WAY WE WERE

"I don't much like piña colada, but I do like getting caught in the rain and if you do too, we are off to a wonderful start."

—A 28-year-old British woman

In her history of American courtship, *From the Front Porch to the Back Seat*, Beth Bailey revisits a time when leaving college without an engagement ring was sometimes thought worse than leaving without a degree. She cites an early 1950s advertisement placed by a Northwestern University sorority in its chapter newspaper: "Seeking Husbands for all A E Phi seniors so they will not graduate a disgrace." Although not every woman who attended college 50 years ago did earn the sought-after "Mrs." degree, the pressure was strong.

Florence, a 70-year-old retired teacher, remembers how even her high school guidance counselor saw college primarily as a way to hook a man. When she approached her senior year with no clear plans about what to do with her life, the guidance counselor advised her to go to college. Florence did some research and finally settled on a nearby state teachers college. Yet when she reported her decision to him, he only frowned. "He told me I should really go to one of the bigger universities so I could meet someone with money."

Florence did manage to find a husband, one of the boys next door to the house she grew up in, but today she is permanently separated. She lives in a world where the Internet has dramatically expanded people's options and allows them to be far more direct in expressing their desires. When Florence grew up, Glenn Miller was singing "Don't Sit Under the Apple Tree," a playful and innocent wartime song echoing the jealousies of departing servicemen and their sweethearts at home. If women who sent their men off to foreign shores during World War II urged them not to sit under the apple tree or hold another on their knee, consider what they must worry about today. A number of online dating services, such as Lavalife and Matchmaker have sections set up specially for members of the military, and hundreds of armed forces members, gay and straight, married and single, are using the Internet to find romance and sex. As the United States prepared to go to war with Iraq at the end of 2002, a 25-year-old man stationed in the Middle East posted an ad saying he was married but interested in a discreet encounter, and a 29-year-old married man at a nearby post went online in search of a ménage à trois. An 18-year-old woman, also stationed in the Middle East, was one of several military people advertising for relationships involving domination and submission.

Most people who lived through World War II have a tamer Internet dating style, saying they want a dance partner, a travel companion, or just a conventional relationship. Florence recently joined their ranks and posted her profile on a couple of dating sites. Generally content with the company of her border collie and her children and grandchildren living near her New Jersey home, she was nonetheless open to possibilities. Despite her limited proficiency with computers, she had fewer reservations than many people half her age as she set up an email account and selected an appealing photo to post. For one thing, Florence likes her cigarettes and said she would not mind knowing more kindred smokers in her increasingly antismoking world. Strict antismoking laws, she said, have made bars and other meeting places much less welcoming than when she was young. In those days, she said, finding a mate was altogether a lot easier. "People met mostly at school, college or in the workplace. Some met at the shore. If you looked half decent in a bathing suit, you had no problem meeting a guy on the beach." At a time when people married much younger and pairing off seemed to occur effortlessly with neighbors, college and the workplace were already viewed as forums for people to broaden their horizons and multiply their pool of potential mates.

Trish McDermott, a Match.com vice president, suggested that college was once like the Internet because it exposed young single people to many potential mates they never would have met otherwise. Of course, McDermott added, being exposed to a few hundred or even a few thousand new people on a single campus hardly compares with the numbers the Internet can provide today.

Many people still find their mates at college, and many others marry coworkers, but things have become more complicated. "Back then, if you dated your boss, he probably didn't worry that you would sue him if he broke up with you," McDermott said. Indeed, the 1966 cult classic *Valley of the Dolls* portrayed post-college life in New York City as a scene utterly free of political correctness where no one worried about mixing business with pleasure. When a girl fresh out of Radcliffe takes a job as a receptionist for a talent agency, her boss is a curious combination of father figure and social liaison who introduces her to a world of carousing until dawn while steering her away from the ladies' men and toward the more marriage-minded types. On her first out-of-town business trip, the young woman sleeps with a client, never stopping to consider that there may be some professional conflict of interest.

The rising stature of women in the workplace and other changes that left men and women settling far away from their home towns may have helped set the scene for more impersonal dating practices. Personal ads, though, actually date back long before Jacqueline Susann painted a quaint yet racy picture of post-college life in post-war New York. The *Peoples Almanac* lists the very first personal ad as coming from England back in 1727, when the never-married Helen Morrison advertised her desire for a companion in *The Manchester Weekly Journal*. That claim is a matter of some debate. In the United States, the University of Mississippi says it has an older personal ad of sorts, a 1722 letter that Sier Chassin, an assistant warehouse keeper in Louisiana, wrote to one of the King of England's ministers, lamenting the lack of marriageable women in his remote territory. The letter essentially asked the minister if he had any young female acquaintances to ship over.

For as long as lonely people had a means of connecting with a larger world, they have, at least on occasion, put their desires into print. And as long as they had the printed word to hide behind, there was the temptation to stretch the truth. Civil War soldiers sometimes placed personal ads, and one 1864 letter from a Union soldier to a woman named Hattie sounds amusingly modern in the way the soldier confesses to embellishing his description of himself. "My true description differs materially from the one therein set forth, and may not please you as well as the one fancy painted," he wrote, "but I thought it was all for fun, therefore, funningly gave a fictitious description."

Personal ads were not always placed in fun. At times when people faced more pressure, sometimes even legal pressure, to be married, and isolated farm life offered few options, such ads could be a last resort. In 1925, a 51-year-old widowed Iowa farmer named Fannie Jones sought to adopt her grandchildren after her daughter died. Because the adoption would not be permitted unless she had a husband, Jones placed an ad and wound up marrying a railroad worker from a neighboring state.

One of the best glimpses of the rural American social scene in the early 1900s comes from the correspondence of Arch McDonald, a western Texas cattle rancher who, judging by the papers he left behind, seems to have been forever single. Almost 20 years' worth of his papers, preserved by Texas Tech University, capture the feeling of lonely isolation that came with the territory in the Wild West. The bulk of the mail McDonald received between 1903 and 1932 were letters addressing his bachelor status, either from concerned relatives asking if they could make some introductions or letters from young women who, like him, lived a hardscrabble existence in a lawless land. One young woman wrote to McDonald about her "step-papa who shot me in the right side with a double-barrel shotgun when I was only 12 years old." Other women got right to the point, stating how it was important to see a photo before they got too deep into the correspondence. "I certainly do admire your good habits and know that you are a true gentleman, though if I could see your picture I could decide better maybe. HaHa," wrote one woman named Violet.

Among McDonald's papers are flyers from various matrimonial clubs, which appear to be the low-tech, early equivalent of today's Internet dating. One such club, called the Merry Maker, sold, for 25 cents, lists of other single people interested in writing letters. "No more lonely hours. With Uncle Sam delivering mail everywhere, you can have and make friends everywhere," said the Merry Maker flyer. It claimed to have members from all over the United States and from all walks of life, "such as bankers, doctors, wealthy widows and widowers, charming maidens, business men and women, hotel owners, farmers and farmerettes, office girls and clerks, lonely nurses, musicians, teachers, housekeepers, store owners and so forth." Another similar group called the Sincere Corresponding

Club focused more specifically on locating spouses with money and claimed in a promotional letter that it had a list of "Thousands of the finest and most attractive, refined, charming and wealthy ladies seeking husbands." The material from the Sincere Corresponding Club, which was based in Valley, Nebraska, shows how some things just never change. Even then it claimed to be a ground-breaking modern service that was abolishing the shame of paying to find love. "There was a time, many years ago, when people thought it something simply awful for a person to secure a wife or a husband through a matrimonial agency. But times have changed," the Sincere Corresponding Club flyer said. Gentlemen applying for membership were asked to complete a short form listing their name, age, height, disposition, temperament, the value of their personal property and the amount, if any, they were due to inherit.

In general these ads were viewed with some skepticism: at best, the only hope for the desperate; at worst, a way of flirting with danger, or death. Helen Morrison's method of searching for love back in 1727 was considered so outrageous that, the story goes, the mayor of Manchester had her committed to a lunatic asylum for four weeks. More than 100 years later, the budding lonely hearts industry suffered a huge public relations crisis when as many as 40 men who responded to such ads became victims of serial killer Belle Gunness, who dismembered their bodies and buried them in flour sacks on her property. A Norwegian immigrant in the early 1900s, Gunness was widowed young and later received at her Indiana farm a succession of middle-aged men, many of whose remains were discovered only after her death. The lonely heart connection was made when one victim's brother showed up with an ad she had placed in a Scandinavian-American newspaper seeking a husband, lover and provider. The brother also brought a letter that had urged one doomed suitor to come with cash. "Change all the cash you have into paper bills, largest denomination you can get, and sew them real good and fast on the inside of your underwear," she wrote. One of the few female serial killers in U.S. history, Gunness came to be known as the black widow of the heartland. And the serial killer/lonely heart connection was not soon forgotten. As recently as 1989, the film *Sea of Love* offered a dark tale of a killer in New York City who found his victims in newspaper ads.

The birth of the modern, socially acceptable personal ad might be traced to January 16, 1957, when New York City's alternative weekly, *The Village Voice*, published the following notice:

> Congenial, ignorant bachelor (30) wants to meet cultured, patient Frenchman for object companionship & conversation.

It was published on a page where *The Village Voice* listed all its random classifieds—a kind of community bulletin board where people posted requests for a variety of things, from rides cross country to rides to the beach. The ignorant bachelor was the first to ever place an ad there for another person, but he did not immediately start a trend. It would be several years before *The Voice* had a regular personals section, although as the 1960s approached, more people were using the miscellaneous ad page to connect with like-minded individuals. Usually, the notices sounded more friendly than romantic or overtly sexual, as they would one day become. One 1960 ad read, "Have scuba equipment and car. Looking to get together with people with some interest in the sport." Romance just may have blossomed between the scuba divers, but if you were single in New York City in the 1960s, you probably had a better chance of meeting a mate *Valley of the Dolls*-style, in the workplace. Help-wanted ads from the same time abound with listings for a girl Friday and other job descriptions either stating or strongly suggesting that the applicant must be a woman, and had better be attractive. One ad sought girls only for part-time hat-check work, and another announced "a groovy job for a swinging gal."

Even though progressive New Yorkers were not yet entirely comfortable looking for love in the newspaper, they were showing a lot of interest in dating services, particularly computer dating.

Anyone who thinks computer dating is a recent development might be charmed to read this 1970 ad for Compatibility, a service that had members fill out questionnaires, then fed the responses into a massive mainframe to locate likely matches:

> *Utilizing the most advanced and sophisticated computer techniques with the IBM 360/16, Compatibility can GUARANTEE you 2 to 10 compatible referrals every 30 days for five full years.*

Hokey as it sounds today, computer technology was new enough at the time that even some very intelligent people had faith in its ability to deliver concrete answers to life's biggest mysteries, like love. The 360 mainframe, unveiled in 1964, had been considered the most important product in IBM's history; it was the first machine capable of processing answers from thousands of lengthy questionnaires and sorting the results according to similar responses. A couple of Harvard students used this technology to establish the first computer dating service in the mid-1960s. Within five years, a few companies like Compatibility had nationwide operations and were charging customers up to $1,000 for five years of matches. John Nash, the mathematical genius whose battle with schizophrenia was chronicled in Sylvia Nassar's biography *A Beautiful Mind*, went on several computer-generated blind dates in the mid-1960s when he was separated from his wife. As quickly as the business came into vogue, though, it faded away amid mounting complaints that not even the most cutting-edge mainframe could locate soul mates. Many people who tried these services complained they relied too much on superficial questions like a person's hair color or musical tastes, while skirting deeper matters like views about religion and sex. Among the yes-or-no questions the Compatibility dating service asked singles were these:

- I believe in God.

- I am generally good-natured and cheerful.

- Long hair and beards are a sign of the breakdown of our society.

The death of computer dating was probably a small victory for personal ads, suggesting that perhaps people knew their own hearts better than any computer. It is a debate that remains at the center of the matchmaking industry today: whether it is better to pay a professional to find a few promising matches or simply pay for a service that will let you pick for yourself from a fat database of single people.

After the computer dating business died down, personal ads gradually assumed a larger place in newspaper classified sections, and in the American consciousness, as the chart-topping success of the song "Escape" in 1979 reflects. In the tune better known as the "Piña Colada Song," Rupert Holmes croons a sweet story about a man who had grown tired of his lady and contacted a woman who had written a dreamy personal ad about getting caught in the rain and making love on the beach at midnight. As anyone who listens to oldies radio knows, the song ended up being not about infidelity, but about true love gone stale and waiting to be revived. It seems that the man's lady had grown tired of him too, since she was the one who had placed the ad in the first place. After an awkward meeting in a bar, the two discovered all sorts of delightful things about each other that they had never noticed before, and fell in love all over again. Promoting romance, true love and mysterious serendipity while steering clear of anything sleazy, the song practically served as a commercial for personal ads.

The reality of the time was a bit different. Personal ads had started to take hold in more and more newspapers and in some specialized publications such as the august *New York Review of Books,* and all had testimonials from happy customers. Some men and women who posted ads were quickly married, and others just went on a lot of dates and said they were pleasantly surprised by the quality of the people they met. But in 1980, many newspapers' personals sections still had a disproportionate representation from swingers, transgender individuals, inmates seeking pen pals and plain old weirdos, like the author of this 1980 ad that ran under the headline Christian Wife Needed:

> I live in the mountainous Northwestern U.S. I have a college degree and am 38 years old. Never been married. I live a rough life with few luxuries. Burn wood for heat in the winter. I am a messy housekeeper. Want a born again Christian wife who recognizes that the husband is the head of a household. Not a divorcee. No nag. Not interested in anyone involved in astrology, ESP, Eastern religions or any other occult form. Must be 18 to 25 years old. Not too fat, not too skinny, looks not of primary importance. Must be at least 5'7" tall. Must be willing to sew, willing to learn to cook on a wood stove, willing to do light farm chores and live a self-sufficient lifestyle in an unpopulated area. Please send two photos of yourself, a short autobiography, list your likes and dislikes and state what God and His Son Jesus Christ mean in your life.

In 1980, John Burson was a successful 28-year-old Washington, D.C., attorney who was rapidly getting ready to settle down. Over the course of the next decade, he tried everything from church socials to dating services and personal ads. "I wanted to get married," he said. "I was not one of those guys who was a bachelor on purpose." Burson, who despite his best efforts remained single almost until the next century, remembers that personal ads still had a stigma in 1980, but came to be more widely accepted ten years later. The change, he believes, came from the people of the baby-boomer generation coming of marrying age en masse, realizing they had not met the right person and resolving to take matters into their own hands. It probably did not hurt that there were a lot more single people around. In 1960, 69.3 percent of all men in the United States over the age of 15, and 65.9 percent of women over 15, were married; those figures fell to 63.2 percent of men and 58.9 percent of women in 1980 and continued to decline to 57.9 percent of men and 54.7 percent of women in 2000, according to the National Marriage Project, based at Rutgers University. Along with people marrying later, there was, throughout the second half of the 20th century, a rising divorce rate that found many people who had pledged "till death do us part" in search of a second life partner. Between 1960 and 2000, the portion of married men in the United States between the age of 35 and 44 fell from 88 percent to 69 percent; for women it dropped from 87.4 percent to 71.6 percent. The rising divorce rate seems to be a self-perpetuating trend, because statistics show that second marriages have a higher rate of failure than first ones.

It was around 1986 that Burson placed his first personal in *Washingtonian* magazine, baring his soul with an ad describing himself as "Ward Cleaver waiting to happen." His reference to the 1950s sitcom that portrayed a squeaky clean nuclear family free of darkness or dysfunction resonated, and Burson received hundreds of responses. He placed the same ad once a year for several more years and typically received enough letters to sort into separate piles based on age, religion and political beliefs. Not that he was entirely calculating. When Burson finally met the woman who would become his wife, he immediately thought to himself that she was so great, he would like her even if she turned out to be a Democrat. "And when I found out that she was a staunch Republican, I thought even better."

If newspaper personals gained acceptance over time, they never seemed to be able to overcome their unfortunate location in the very back of the paper, not far from the ads for far-out diet schemes, phone sex lines and escort services. Casual readers and even customers of these services often were confused about where the good clean socializing ended and the shady stuff began—when advertising for a date meant "a date" and when it meant an illegal payment for sex. Even the most aboveboard ads seemed to be tarnished by association. One legitimate escort service in Washington, D.C. discovered how hard it was to shake this dicey image when its male customers began calling the police to complain that the companions they had hired did nothing more than talk. One angry customer released a canister of tear gas outside the service's office, and other frustrated men would show up night and day, screaming demands for a refund.

Before it was an Internet dating service, the Canadian company Lavalife operated a telephone personals business, where, beginning in 1987, people could call an 800 number and hear listings for singles that were sorted by age and location. The software that enabled such a service was cutting-edge at the time, predating general voice mail. Still, says Lavalife Executive Chairman Bruce Croxon, it attracted a lot of people looking for kinky sex, or people who just assumed that telephone personals meant phone sex. "You always get that because it is a discreet service, and, at least initially, that is who it attracts," he said. "Our ad campaigns were always about meeting the love of your life, but the people who were using it were often looking for one-night stands, or phone sex, or had some kind of fetish." Lavalife today still runs a popular telephone personals business that has gradually attracted an audience more representative of the general population. Still, its Internet business is experiencing much faster growth. When Lavalife expanded into Internet personals, Croxon recalls it was immediately apparent that both the caliber of customers and the overall reach of the business had changed and grown.

John Burson was 46 when his June Cleaver showed up, and by that time he had moved beyond the personals to other dating strategies. After he turned 40, he focused on meeting people in person rather than through ads; his theory was that women who might be turned off by his age in print would be charmed by his youthful demeanor if they saw him in the flesh. After all his efforts, his future wife literally showed up at his doorstep to attend a massive holiday party at his house. Today Burson looks back with relief that his days of 100 dates in a year, in one case 23 consecutive nights of first dates, are behind him. But he still adheres to the theory that finding love is not so much a matter of destiny as a numbers game. Now a happily married father who basks in the glow of contentment and wishes the rest of the world could share his good fortune, he urges single friends and family members to try Internet dating, which he thinks is better than any of the tools he used to have to work with. On the Internet, he argues, you can search a much broader cross section of potential mates, search worldwide if you wish, and then immediately start an email correspondence, rather than sending a letter via snail mail off to some anonymous post office box and waiting for a response from the person in the newspaper ad.

This promise of increased benefits linked to scale was recognized at the peak of the dot-com boom by some companies like Nerve.com, which operates a Web site devoted to the intelligent discussion of sex—a kind of *Playboy* for intellectuals, complete with online personals. In 2000 Nerve cofounder Rufus Griscom offered the television news magazine *60 Minutes* this vision of the online dating future: "You will be able to go online and say, 'I'm looking for someone who loves Faulkner, hates their mother, lives in rural Mississippi, is 5' 11", has green eyes,' and 500 different people come up on the screen." Even in the context of those heady times, it sounded like one of the more outrageous claims being put forth. Griscom's vision, as literally described, has not come true, but the general flavor of the forecast was somewhat accurate.

The breadth and diversity of people online is illustrated by the experience of one 35-year-old bisexual Muslim woman who recently posted her profile online, saying she had red hair, multiple tattoos and a plump body. Within one hour she had heard from two interested suitors in the same small Bible Belt city where she lived. The staggering numbers of singles online can serve more plain-vanilla types too. Burson said he has a relative who used to travel a lot for work and used the Internet to line up dates in advance in cities where he had business trips.

Burson did not know it at the time, but online dating had been an option during many of his single years. John Boede is an Internet industry executive who met his very first girlfriend online all the way back in 1985 after he and his buddy Scott Smith set up a crude dating site in San Antonio, Texas. It was at a time when the general public still had little knowledge of the Internet, but groups of computer workers and all-around geeks were beginning to get a kick out of the idea that one computer could talk to another. Lots of bulletin boards were set up to connect little groups of hobbyists, but from the outset, the meeting site Boede and Smith built, called Matchmaker, was unusually popular. It received more than double the traffic of any other computer bulletin board in San Antonio even though the male/female ratio on the Internet in those days was at least five-to-one.

The small dating site endured, and today it is Matchmaker.com, a part of the Internet media site Lycos.com. Boede serves as chief programmer for Matchmaker, which signs up about 200,000 new members a month. As it has grown, Matchmaker has built itself into an unusually detail-oriented site, where people register not just their age, weight and hair color, but fill out a lengthy survey including their thoughts on dancing, money and body art, and even the form of transportation they use to get around town. The process seems designed not just to collect detail, but to help people convey their own individual sense of style and sense of humor, sight unseen. Under the question about one's style of hair, for instance, are some 20 choices, ranging from long straight hair and short curly hair, to Mohawk, dreadlocks, "bald on top with a fringe," "toupee or not toupee," "I spray paint my head," and finally, "my hair defies description." Perhaps a few too many options for the man with short straight hair who likes women with long curly hair, but Boede argues that this survey reflects one of the big advantages the Internet offers over newspaper ads: letting people show how they are different from all the other single white females without breaking the bank in the process. Newspaper personal ads, after all, are only cheap for people who have a great economy with words. In 1979, that whimsical "if you like piña coladas" ad would have run about $67.50 in an upscale magazine, not to mention a $10 or $15 fee for the anonymous post office box.

"We had some awful press coverage in the early days. The editors would always turn the story into something like, Computer Nerds Need Love Too," said Boede. "But it was clear to us we were on to something. We were one of the few bulletin boards that actually had women calling in." Although Boede ultimately broke up with his Internet girlfriend and met the woman who would become his wife offline, at a winery, he was sold on the business by the success stories of so many others. "I've watched many people over the years find absolutely the perfect person for them online," he said, dismissing the still persistent notion that such sites cater to people on the margins of society. "So many people say, 'I would have never found this person otherwise.' I've had that drilled into my head a thousand times."

To be fair, many early adopters were, to put it gently, a little on the shy side or a little on the sleazy side. No matter all the attractive and socially well-adjusted types who went online simply to try something new, the Internet could not help but become a haven for people too awkward or too "out there" to socialize with ease in the real world. Throughout the 1990s, as computer and Internet use exploded and the computer-book industry flourished, so too did a niche publishing section focused on online flirting and dating. At least three separate books called *The Joy of Cybersex* were published during the 1990s. While the title they all shared might suggest they were written for a hip, sexually experimental crowd, their text is more geared toward people who struggle with basic pickup lines, the very kind of outcast so many people worried they might end up with if they resorted to the personals. In the 1998 book *The Joy of Cybersex*, author Deb Levine seemed to write for that quintessential computer geek who looked at the cracks on the sidewalk when he walked down the street and considered bathing optional. "Everyone says you have to be out there in order to meet your special someone," she counseled. "And you have to risk rejection in order to enjoy the possibility of being accepted. They're right. But what if you can't bear the thought of walking up to a stranger, no less an attractive one, and saying something clever off the top of your head?" The solution, wrote Levine, was simply to spend more time online. "The anonymity creates an environment where you can make mistakes without feeling embarrassed or ashamed. No one will ever know if you haven't slept a wink, if you have stubble on your face, or if you haven't put on your makeup yet. In addition to not having to worry about looking your best, the anonymity also means you never have to see a particular person again if you flub it."

There was a separate audience for these Internet sex books, but it was equally far from the mainstream. The group that Nancy Tamosaitis focused on in her 1995 book *Net.Sex* is best illustrated by the book's index. Under B, the index lists bestiality and bondage; H, the hair-fetish forum; I, infantilism; and N, the North American Man-Boy Love Association (NAMBLA). "Some men and women believe the best type of sex is with a beautiful, willing partner and no commitment," the author wrote. "That is what happens every time a person has cybersex. You can imagine what the digital lover looks like, and how he or she will sound and act. And you don't even have to make them breakfast the next day."

Growing Internet use by both men and women through the 1990s gradually helped make the dating sites more of a true cross section of society, but there was another factor speeding adoption: the roaring economy. The same giddy environment that had left the 27-year-old HotOrNot founder James Hong happily spending his free evenings attending business discussions with other would-be entrepreneurs had spread across the country by 2000, enticing young and not-so-young professionals to cool it on the social front and get down to work. As stock prices continued to rise, people everywhere were losing the nine-to-five, retire at 65 mentality and devising get-rich-quick schemes. They had seen other people make money on investments, through day trading or on stock options issued by their employers, and they wanted to get in on the ground floor somewhere while this window to wealth was still open. Many people in their prime dating years willingly swapped hours of carefree downtime for late nights at the office, and media accounts of the dot-com boom say as much about the sad social style of the young and ambitious as they do about their style of doing business.

Typical of the time was Calvin Lui, the 27-year-old founder of a Web site called TheMan.com, one of many Internet startups in San Francisco that failed almost before it launched in 1999. TheMan was supposed to be a site where clueless guys could get advice about dating, and shop for the perfect gift for their sweeties; the irony was that its founders were too busy for girls. In 1999, while company engineers were hard at work on the preposterous project of building an algorithm that would calculate the best date based on the type of girl being courted, Lui boasted to *Time* magazine that he had only had one date all summer. That night out, he maintained, had been only for research. He did not say if he had found his date on the Internet, but such an efficient means of searching would have suited his businesslike style. Around the same time, another high-tech company founder also in his twenties boasted that work had become so exciting that dates bored him, and a third said that he rationed himself to four hours sleep per night so that he would have more time to put in at the office.

Such lifestyles helped fuel an attitude that dating was not so much a leisure activity as something you put on your to-do list. Today, although offline dating services have lost some ground to the Internet, they say they have benefited from a society where people are less embarrassed than ever to express even their most personal needs. "People are a lot more open and accepting of the fact that it is a fast-paced world and we need help with a variety of things, from a psychiatrist, to a mechanic who drops you off and picks you up, to a dating service," said Steve Dubin, a spokesman for Together, one of the largest offline dating services in the United States. Katie Mitic, who heads Yahoo Personals and has years of experience working for high-paced Internet startup companies, puts it more bluntly. "Online dating," she says, "brings time-saving efficiencies by allowing a person to manage several prospects simultaneously."

In the end, pop culture was also a huge factor in getting the ball rolling on this new trend. In 1998, *You've Got Mail* became the first major comedy about a romance born online. A happy, perky film that showed two attractive professionals revealing their deepest thoughts to each other through an online chat room, the film worked wonders in erasing negative stereotypes—so much so that at least one Wall Street analyst said he upgraded some Internet stocks after seeing the film in New York City and overhearing numerous people saying as they left the theater that they really ought to try this Internet thing.

3

WHAT PRICE LOVE?

*"I'm looking for a very rich lady who loves to spend money
and is very beautiful, and loves to play tennis. I don't
think that's asking for too much, do you?"*

— A 44-year-old New York man

It was during a rather low point in her social life when Olivia, a woman in her thirties living outside Boston, noticed an ad for a free trial membership to an Internet dating service called Date.com. She visited the company's Web site, where she read testimonials from happy couples who had met through its service, as well as promises for something more than just random matching. "Date.com was not designed by system engineers," the site said. "It is the work of relationship experts, psychologists, and communications professionals. Date.com features a secret matching algorithm which is as closely guarded a secret as the formula for Coca-Cola." Figuring she had nothing to lose, Olivia tried the free membership. "I guess it looked fun, and I was just bored enough to go for it. I live in a very,

33

very small town. Dating is tough here because everyone knows everyone, they all grew up together, went to school together, dated each other, had children by each other and are related, either by blood or marriage. By comparison," said Olivia, "Date.com looked like a pretty sweet deal."

By the time she registered and began to hear from some men on the site, though, the free part of the membership had expired and she was asked to pay a monthly fee if she wished to continue any of her correspondences. She paid the money, but soon became skeptical about Date.com's supposed secret sauce for making matches. Olivia wanted a serious relationship; most of the men she heard from were decidedly more casual. "Many were just looking to hook up and sent crude notes. So, I decided just to close the account," she said. That was when her online dating experience really went downhill. She contacted Date.com via email to terminate her membership, but charges continued to show up on her credit card. She called a customer service line and left a voicemail, but no one got back to her. Again she tried calling, again no response. "I was only there for three months," she recalled several months later. "But I spent almost that long trying to get out. Their customer service department seemed to be a phantom email address. I wrote two or three times a week. No confirmation they had ever received my complaints. I began sweetly, but by the end, Armageddon, Armageddon!"

Then, just as her story of frustration seemed to be reaching its peak, Olivia's tone softened. "I did meet someone nice, though," she added.

Olivia's experience of horrible customer service coupled with finding just what she wanted in spite of it all is odd for any business. It also says a lot about why so many businesses have been able to make some quick money on Internet dating. Slap up even the most bare-bones Web site where people can go to look for love, and odds are, some of those people will find it. People fall in love all the time in free online chat rooms set up to host discussions on cooking, pets or travel. This is bound to happen more when a Web site sets itself up as a romance destination. Today, some of the larger dating services are investing heavily to build sites that don't crash and have superior searching technology for zeroing in on the red-headed Muslim women living in the Bible Belt, or mom-hating Faulkner fans from rural Mississippi, but that is just icing. Even a site like Date.com, which is unable to produce evidence that it has any matching standards at all (let alone a secret matching algorithm) and which frequently fails to respond to billing and customer service questions, has a lot of satisfied customers. The company seems to recognize, too, that one or two stories of true love found on its site can go a long way toward masking other lapses. Shortly before Valentine's Day, a public relations representative for the company tried to sell journalists on the story of Phil, a 40-year-old Seattle resident who met his future wife on Date.com one day when he was home sick with pneumonia. "I thought it would make a great story," she gushed in an email that drew parallels to the romantic comedy *Sleepless in Seattle*. Yet when one reporter came back to her with some broader questions about Date.com—how large was its customer staff, and what was this secret matching algorithm all about anyway—she no longer wanted to talk. "Unfortunately, Date.com will not be able to participate in this opportunity," she wrote in a curt response. Despite several requests, Date.com has never elaborated on its supposed matching algorithm.

Even those dating sites that don't cut any corners seem to have it easier than many other Internet businesses. Their costs may be steep, but they are somewhat fixed once a critical mass of subscribers is reached. Match.com's Chief Technology Officer, Mike Presz, oversees the company's single largest department; his team works round the clock to keep the site running smoothly. But he says that with the amount of high-tech manpower onboard now, Match.com could double its eight million-plus membership and not have to expand its staff. This matter of fixed costs is a key factor that separated companies like the online auction site eBay from the online retail site Amazon.com, and so many other labor- or equipment-intensive Internet businesses. One of the few consumer Internet businesses comfortably profitable today, eBay is a site that really only exists to connect buyers and sellers. It never had to invest in warehouses to store merchandise, nor in personnel to handle shipping or returns. More than $18 billion worth of merchandise is sold over its site in a year, but that is all done by third parties; eBay is just the middleman. Online dating services play a similar role. Match.com charges members $24.95 for one month's access to all the single people on its site; at Yahoo Personals and most of the other major dating sites, the fee is about the same. Subscribers must pay the fee to make initial contact with other singles on the site, but after that they are on their own to meet and greet. Like eBay, the dating sites play the lucrative role of middleman.

The online dating business has something else going for it: a nifty subscription model that has a way of keeping members hooked. You don't have to pay anything to belong to eBay, just come and go as the mood strikes you, and pay a fee only when you complete a sale. Although a couple of dating services such as Lavalife operate with the same kind of transaction-based fee structure, most sell one-month, three-month and even one-year subscriptions. It is sort of the equivalent of an all-you-can-eat offer at a restaurant, enabling you to contact and date as many people as time permits. People often remark that you would have to be pretty pessimistic to buy a one-year subscription, to commit yourself to the unattached dating life for a full 12 months, but many inadvertently wind up staying that long. Use your credit card to buy a one-month subscription to Match.com, and you will automatically be charged for a second month, unless you remember to cancel your subscription. You will also get charged for a whole second month if you go to the site a day late to cancel. Some sites further require subscribers make an actual phone call to customer service to cancel. That could mean waiting until the customer service office is open the next morning, and by then, incurring another full month charge. So you wind up staying for a second month, and then, just as you are about to cancel for good, on day 30 of month two, you hear from someone who sounds swell. You never know, you think to yourself, you might as well write back. But you can't unless you keep your membership active. And so your subscription is extended for a third month.

It was during some of the darkest days for Yahoo that the company started to consider how much money it could make from a subscription-based personals service. Yahoo, the Internet media site that set out to be the place where anyone could find any kind of information, had offered personals on its site for years, but the service had always been free. Its main function had been regarded as a way to attract more people, or eyeballs, as they were called in the lingo of the day. Until the middle of 2000 or so, Yahoo's whole business model had been based on selling advertising. More eyeballs meant higher ad rates. Then stock prices started to collapse, dot-com companies ran out of money and started closing up shop, and Yahoo began to understand that what had looked like a rock-solid base of loyal advertisers was really just a shaky group of startup companies. It tried to attract ad dollars from the kinds of companies that had been around for 100 years and were not going to go away tomorrow—car companies and entertainment companies, fast food companies and soap companies—but by then the country was in a recession and everyone was being cautious about discretionary marketing spending. Yahoo realized it had better stop giving away all its services for free. In an effort to offset the devastating loss of advertising dollars, it began slapping fees on a variety of services such as games, retrieval of documents not generally available on the Web and its online payment services. In 2001 it added a fee to its popular personals service.

In most senses the strategy has been a success. By the summer of 2002, Yahoo had broken a six-quarter losing streak and was crediting its new fees and listings business for the return to profitability. The company said it had collected money from one million customers whose payments for things such as bigger email boxes or access to one of the biggest pools of single people on the Web had contributed 40 percent to total company revenues. Six months later, Yahoo was really on a roll. It ended 2002 with 2.2 million paying subscribers. But what were all those people subscribing to? Probably not the document retrieval service. The company admits that just a few of its services, including expanded email and online personals, are generating the bulk of subscriber fees. To offer a sense for how aggressively Yahoo has promoted its personals business, in 2002 it ran ads, worth an estimated $325.9 million, for Yahoo Personals on its own Web site, according to Evaliant, which tracks advertising industry data. Because they were house ads, Yahoo did not have to actually pay for them, but it was a staggering amount that suggested Yahoo Personals could be bigger than any other advertiser on Yahoo. The nearly $326 million worth of house ads for Yahoo Personals is more than a third of the company's total revenues that year.

This resounding success of Yahoo Personals puts Yahoo, the online media empire, in a rather curious position. On the one hand, it is happy to admit that charging money for personals was one of the smartest things it ever did. But it would probably rather not be defined as a dating destination. The solution seems to be to keep everything a little bit vague. Yahoo will not say which service brings in the most fees—only that personals and email storage are the top two. Several industry analysts, though, suspect the personals business holds the top slot. "It's got to be the biggest," said James Preissler, an analyst at Investec. "My guess is that they have 400,000 to 500,000 subscribers." The executives at Yahoo may not have been thinking about things like synergy when they began adding fees, but the company's expanded email and its personals business may, in a curious way, be supporting each other. More dating online means more mail in your inbox, and ultimately, more demand for a bigger box.

Around the same time that Yahoo went through its identity crisis, its smaller rival, Terra Lycos, was running into all the same problems and pursuing the same solutions. In 2000, as part of a broader strategy to sign up more paying customers, the company acquired the Matchmaker.com dating site. Today, thousands of new members post profiles on Matchmaker each day, and the company claims to receive roughly 100 pieces of fan mail a month from people who found their life partner on that site. "Our biggest premium service is the dating service," said Meredith Hanrahan, vice president of entertainment content for Terra Lycos. Hanrahan said that Matchmaker, after years of enjoying a cult following, has started to see an explosion in interest as word-of-mouth referrals reach a crescendo. She estimates that as recently as the end of 1999, only about 2 percent of adult singles in the United States were using online personals sites. "Today it is anywhere between 20 and 25 percent of singles who are using it," she said.

Before so many Internet companies became focused on the lucrative but basically old-fashioned personals business, they all seemed to have more important matters on their agendas. Back when Lycos.com was still a high-flying Internet site, before it was bought by the Spanish media company Terra Networks and before it had to scramble to generate revenues, it was turning away takeover offers. In early 1999, when the Internet bubble had swelled just about to capacity and businesses of all sorts were putting ".com" after their names, the broadcasting company USA Networks tried to buy Lycos. At the time, USA Networks was best known for its core asset, Home Shopping Network, and Lycos was one of the top five Internet portals, some months even ranking a close second behind Yahoo. USA Networks, in other words, was seen as a favorite of little old homebound ladies, while Lycos, the thinking went, had its best days ahead of it. Lycos had recently been spun off by CMGI, which at the time was a respected incubator of dot-com companies that had a collection of young Internet businesses in its portfolio—and one of the fastest-rising stock prices on Wall Street. *Red Herring* magazine, which chronicled all the deal-making going on in the Internet industry, described CMGI as "an Oz-like wonderland of pre-IPO companies with a tangled web of synergies." Its saccharine tone was pretty typical of the time. The USA Networks acquisition of Lycos never went through, essentially because everyone seemed to think Lycos could do better. "Frankly, USA Networks needs Lycos more than Lycos needs USA Networks," Internet stock fund manager Ryan Jacobs remarked at the time. CMGI hemmed and hawed about the USA Networks bid, but it was obvious that company executives were thinking that Lycos really did not need to align itself with a company that sold cubic zirconia over the television. USA Networks Chief Barry Diller finally threw in the towel, and a year later Lycos was acquired by Terra Networks.

It has been a rough few years for all parties involved. Terra Lycos today is a struggling online media business, and CMGI has endured a pretty steady downhill battle to salvage what often looks more like a wasteland than a wonderland of Internet investments. But Diller's company is not doing half badly. At the end of 2002 it acquired Ticketmaster, and with that came the Ticketmaster subsidiary Match.com. That deal capped a series of transactions that has gradually expanded the company's Internet presence, but only in a narrow way. Most of USA Networks' Internet assets today, like the online travel site Expedia.com, the ticket-selling site Ticketmaster.com and Match.com, are businesses that function as middlemen and enjoy relatively fixed costs. Although Match.com represents a small part of total company revenues, it is representative of the larger strategy for the company, which later changed its name to USA Interactive and today is known as Interactive Inc. "It is a very simple notion," suggests UBS Warburg analyst Christopher Dixon. "The Internet is really good at disintermediating processes. Disintermediating the process is just taking out the intermediary and the easiest one to do this in is dating." Dixon said the company's involvement with Match.com is the epitome of this strategy. "The most important thing Match.com has done for USA Interactive is not so much its financial impact on the company but the recognition that there were other processes out there that the Internet could help facilitate." Although no one talked much about the online dating business back in 1999 when Diller's company was courting Lycos, today Terra Lycos and USA Interactive are rivals in this fast-growing business, which appears to offer clear value over the offline model. "Online dating is one of the few revenue models that really works online," said Lycos's Hanrahan. "You can access it 24/7 for a reasonable fee, whereas an offline dating service might cost you $1,500 or $1,600."

Actually, $1,500 is not even a particularly high fee for some offline dating services, which today find themselves pressed to prove they offer more value than their cheaper online rivals. Before the online personals became a phenomenon that many people freely admitted to using, matchmaking had been a guarded and private industry. There are many offline services that host singles events or arrange one-on-one introductions; one called TheraDate even matches up people who are seeking psychological counseling. But few of these services will quote rates. Critics argue that is because they prefer to use hard-sell tactics and prey on the single person's sense of desperation once he is in the office. Angelo DiMeglio, a builder and contractor who lives in Massachusetts, said he once visited the Boston office of Great Expectations, a nationwide dating service, and managed within five minutes to talk down the price of an 18-month membership from $3,000 to $795.

According to people who have joined such services, though, they usually cost at least $1,000. Table For Six, a San Francisco service that organizes intimate dinners with three single men and three single women around the same table, charges about $1,600 for a yearly membership, dinner not included. Once upon a time, that may have looked like a great deal. If you were diligent and went on a dinner every single week of the year, you would meet 156 people of the opposite sex—a not exorbitant $10 per introduction. Online dating sites, though, are upsetting the scale, because most make it easy to scan 156 profiles from the comfort of your home in a single evening.

It is not just the limited quantity that has left some customers unhappy. Danielle, a 33-year-old college administrator on the West Coast, paid $1,300 for 10 introductions through a service called It's Just Lunch, which promised a discreet and confidential discernment process to get to the core of what she wanted in a man. She was so dissatisfied with the service, however, that she only made it to three dates. Danielle recalls that her screening interview was with a woman who was "brusque, rude and not at all sensitive to confidentiality issues," who conducted an interview consisting entirely of "ridiculous, superficial questions" that were not likely to get to the core of her character. Moreover, she said, they did not seem to even listen to her answers to the superficial questions. Danielle had specified that she wanted to meet only men who were 5'9" or taller; after she wrote the check, an intern informed her that they had no tall guys among their clientele. In fact, said Danielle, it appeared to her that college interns who had not even participated in the initial matchmaking were the ones setting her up on dates. "It was so humiliating," she said. "I could have walked into the grocery store and found better people myself."

Valenti International is a high-end matchmaking service that says its clients are educated, cultured, polo-playing types who are too busy to find mates on their own. Like most agencies of this sort, Valenti would never do anything so crass as publish its rates, but an associate for the company said it typically charges a $10,000 retainer fee, and another $10,000 finder fee if the matchmaking efforts result in a marriage. Overweight people, he said, must pay a little extra. And what does one get for that $10,000? As it is with the fees, the company is a little bit vague about services rendered. In promotional material and in discussions with prospective clients, Valenti touts its rigorous psychological profiling and the 24-hour fax line it operates for members to submit feedback forms after dates. The community newspaper in the company's hometown of Rancho Santa Fe, California, says Valenti also provides image consulting and referrals to plastic surgeons. But, aside from advising clients to go under the knife, it is difficult to know, without paying the hefty fee, what level of personal attention you will get for your money, and whether such high-priced matchmakers really do have a valuable skill. "The people we deal with are not the kinds of people who join online dating services," the company associate said. "We generally have doctors, CEOs and lawyers among our clientele. The people who join online dating services are desperate and flaky."

This type of attack has become more common as online dating sites offer a low-cost alternative and the older, more expensive operations counter with an argument about quality over quantity. Yet both sides seem to be enjoying some of the benefits of an explosion in matchmaking of all kinds. Marketdata Enterprises estimated that at the end of 2002, matchmaking online and off had become a $917 million business in the United States, showing growth of more than 50 percent since 1998. Whether more people are getting divorced, fewer are finding mates in college or there is some other demographic trend, everyone seems to agree that the broad acceptance of online dating sites has made people more willing to admit they need some help in the love department. Marketdata said that the offline chains and franchises such as Great Expectations and other services that typically charge around $3,000 are also growing, catering to singles who want background checks on potential mates and a generally more personalized approach.

Is there not something to be said for paying an experienced professional to screen prospects for you, to reduce the pool to just a promising few, so you don't waste your time? Pat Moore would argue yes. For 15 years until her retirement a few years ago, Moore operated The Pat Moore Group, an upscale matchmaking service in northern California that boasted an unusually high success rate of 25 percent. One-quarter of all of her customers, who paid $5,000 for a year of introductions, ended up marrying a match she found for them. As Moore remembers, matchmaking was an inexact science in which people either did not understand what they were looking for or had a very hard time articulating it. "I would have people come in and they would literally hand me a list of 15 qualities they wanted. The lists would all be the same," she said, yawning as she recalled all the repetition. "Sense of humor, appreciation of the arts, good value system, able to relax and have fun, but at the same time be serious." Clients who went to Moore, like those who today go to Valenti, would fill out lengthy questionnaires and have files built around the feedback from their dates. "The kind of matchmaking I did was very time-involving," she said. "You had to get to know each person very well. As you refine the information you will eventually reach the place where you can see how they will react to different people. But that takes time and they usually have to date several people first."

In all her time in the business, Moore said she produced just a single instant match in which one client married the very first person she met through her service. Other times, her intuition was way off. She introduced an Armenian man from northern California to an Armenian woman from southern California, who, after entertaining each other for a marathon 10-hour phone call, decided it was safe to meet. "They took one look at each other and he took the next plane back," said Moore, who found that the experience underscored how physical appearance was as critical as emotional chemistry. Advocates of online dating services, which often feature members' photos argue the ability to screen images from home saves them the time of meeting a person they will know from first glance is wrong, but Moore disagrees. In her practice, no client was ever allowed to see photos of possible dates prior to meeting. "You don't know what a person looks like until you have sat down and talked to them," she said. "If they have a self-assurance, a sense of humor, just an appreciation of living in this world, all those things can come out in a person's appearance after you have talked for a while."

Yet after a long and successful career, Moore can't really pinpoint how she went about producing her matches, and one is left wondering whether her 25 percent success rate was the result of skill or just came from the promising odds she started with when she put together a group of educated and affluent marriage-minded men and women. Her matchmaking stories are interesting, but they really do not resolve the question of whether skill and intuition are more valuable than a large database of people you can find online. "What skills did I use? Well, my degree is in cultural anthropology," she offered. "I always felt that if your value systems were in line you had a pretty good bet." That's it? That's all your $5,000 would get you, some screening for similar value systems? "Well, beyond a certain number of criteria, it is sort of inexact. On the other hand, I wouldn't introduce a devout Catholic to an Orthodox Jew," she tried again.

There is one aspect of the business where Moore will confess she was limited. In order to keep personal control over the process, she would work with no more than 400 clients at a time. Their fees of $5,000 apiece made for some healthy cash flow, but large chunks of that went right back out to advertising. "You get a lot of money coming in, but the net is pretty low," Moore said, adding that the labor-intensive nature of the business made it impossible to take advantage of scale in the way that more impersonal online sites can. Today, some offline matchmakers are themselves dipping into the online dating pool. Jill Kelleher, who operates an upscale matchmaking service, said when she gets a client who lives in an out-of-the-way place or is for some other reason a particularly tough match, she will sometimes search for matches on Match.com.

It has been several years since entrepreneurs in Silicon Valley and New York were really enthused about the Internet, and now that hysteria seems to have reached upstate New York. The Ithaca, New York, office of a new dating site called GreatBoyfriends.com is almost shrill with enthusiasm. It is 2003, online dating is all the rage and Cande Carroll and her sister E. Jean (pronounced Candy and, well, E. Jean) have come up with a new concept that blends the personal touch of old-fashioned matchmaking with the efficiency and scale of the Internet. Their fledgling Web site offers this clever slogan: "GreatBoyfriends.com: Where every single man comes with a woman's stamp of approval."

All the men profiled on GreatBoyfriends were put there by a woman: a sister, a mother, even an old girlfriend who always thought her ex would be perfect for someone, just not her. Like every other dating site, GreatBoyfriends plans to eventually start charging money for its service, but at the moment it is handing out free memberships to any women who will recommend a man. The site has barely gotten off the ground, but everyone seems to be intrigued with this idea of bringing a little yenta-like influence to the Internet dating scene. The media loves the GreatBoyfriends site, and the site founders think all the attention can only bode well. "There are times when we get very caught up in the growth of our little baby site here, and it really is just a teeny little site, but it is tremendously thrilling to see, our big days of growth ahead of us," Cande Carroll says with a childlike enthusiasm that sounds very 1999. Judging from the noise in the background, the business is operating a bare-bones 1999-style startup office too. Carroll's voice is repeatedly interrupted by the kind of caller ID clicks you get when you have only one phone line. That hasn't stopped her from thinking big. "Girls feel it is safe and trustworthy," she says. "And big media is saying it is trustworthy. *The New York Times*, The CBS Morning News, The Today Show..." GreatBoyfriends.com was a media favorite of Valentine's Day 2003, but in fact it is just one of a string of smaller sites launched in recent years, all set up by people who either had a vision of transforming the dating process, or just a vision of making some money. It was a little bit of both for Sue Bergin, an unmarried writing instructor at Brigham Young University in Provo, Utah, who in 1999 saw a need for a more serious dating service and decided it would be pretty simple to set up a dating site herself. She designed SinglesWithScruples.com, which played up values and decency and tried to reduce the emphasis on wealth and material possession that Bergin said she had noticed on so many of the big dating sites. Effortlessly, Bergin attracted an audience of several thousand, and then she started hearing from married couples who had met on her little site. But almost four years later, Bergin has not been able to quit her day job. (She is also still single.) Because she refused to collect money until the site was bug-free, she did not charge any subscriber fees for a long time. Many of the people who met on her site and later married made their connection without even paying the modest $12 monthly charge she later imposed. "It was actually much more difficult than I thought," Bergin says today. "I had no idea how much of a pain it would be, getting a good programmer and things like that. I went through a number of teams and it was a nightmare."

The technological challenge of running a site is only one of the factors separating the GreatBoyfriends and SinglesWithScruples of the Internet from the industry leaders like Match.com. Linda Woods, a consultant who has carved out a successful business advising companies on affiliate marketing opportunities, argues that it is hard to underestimate the money and labor involved in selling your Internet service, even if you have a dating site that claims to grow by word of mouth. "When you are as big as Match.com, word of mouth referrals," she says, "simply are not going to sustain you."

"The hardest thing about starting a dating site is getting a database," said Woods, whose company, Affiliate Goddess, advises Internet businesses on how to get partner Web sites to work for them. Affiliate marketing online is essentially the practice of placing banners for one company's Web site all over the Web to help drive traffic—the online equivalent, says Woods, of the teams of Tupperware salespeople that fan out across suburbia. Although affiliate marketing programs once were widely misused by companies that paid too much for the Web traffic sent their way, Woods says Match.com today operates one of the most successful affiliate marketing programs on the Internet. The company, which has teamed up with such unlikely partners as Weather.com and even advertises on rival dating sites such as Nerve.com, says it sees affiliate marketing as an effective soft sell for people who would never initiate a visit to a dating site, but just may click a banner when it is placed in front of them. Like a banner for a diet service, these links enable people to seek help without coming right out and admitting they have a problem. Match.com currently pays its affiliate partners a "bounty fee" of at least $10 for every $24.99 monthly membership they produce. That is a seemingly staggering finder's fee of 40 percent for basically no real labor on the part of the affiliate. Woods insists, however, that Match.com is the big winner in such arrangements, because subscribers to online dating services stay for an average of six months.

Sites such as Match.com, in other words, may truly want you to find just what you are looking for. It's just that they make a lot more money when your search lasts for six months, rather than three. As online dating has attracted more attention from serious business people, some have come up with another parallel besides that of the ultra-successful online auction industry. In several respects, online dating is more akin to the online job search business, today dominated by sites such as Monster.com and Hot-Jobs.com. Like the personals business, recruiting became a much more high-profile business when it moved from the back of news-papers to the Internet. That shift has greatly expanded the options of job seekers and employers, who once were more likely to look within a narrow geographic area. HotJobs saw so much potential to grow its business that in 1999 it spent half of its revenues from the prior year to buy one single ad to air during the Super Bowl. And in 2001, Yahoo purchased HotJobs as part of its effort to build more consistent revenue streams. Yet today some of that promise has faded. The most immediate problem is the cyclical nature of the recruiting business, which by 2002 was suffering from the overall job shortage. There is no clear indication that the personals business is also cyclical, although some San Francisco personals sites reported that dating activity actually went up as the economy went south.

Yet Investec analyst James Preissler points out that online recruiting and online dating sites also share a big challenge. When they produce a happy customer, either by filling a job or delivering a mate, that customer is gone. Being in either of these businesses means constantly having to scramble for new customers. "It is an industry that is rife with churn," Preissler says of the dating busi-ness. Moreover, Monster.com Chief Executive Jeff Taylor acknowl-edges that job seekers who a few years ago were wowed by the wealth of possibilities online are more likely today to seek a happy medium between expanding their horizons and sticking to familiar territory close to home. Just because they have access to a literal world of opportunities does not mean they want to pursue them all. To continue the parallel to the online dating scene, singles too could conclude, once they get past the kid-in-a-candy-store thrill, that it is not necessarily helpful to have an infinite list of possibili-ties before them.

As online dating sites try to make more money, some are con-sidering ways to retain subscribers for longer periods of time. Spring Street Networks, whose fast-growing personals service is used by many Web content companies and alternative weekly newspapers such as *The Village Voice*, says it is careful to bill its service as more than just a place to find a spouse. "We think of it as more of an entertainment service," said a spokesman. "The flirting, the fun people have is actually the bigger business. People certainly use our service to marry or find long-term relationships, but we also try to create an environment where it is fun, where you can meet a lot of Mr. 98 Percent Rights."

Against this problem of customer churn is the possibly bigger challenge of getting customers to pay in the first place. If Internet dating has become relatively mainstream, the majority of singles in the United States are either still not comfortable using a dating service, or are not comfortable paying for it. Jill is a single 30-year-old from Salt Lake City who went so far as to post a profile on Match.com, but did not see anything to convince her she should pay to subscribe. "I have heard from about seven guys in response to my profile," she said. "But I am apprehensive about emailing any of them back. They all sound a little weird." Caroline is a 27-year-old living in Connecticut who has a serious boyfriend and no real interest in going on dates with new men. She posted her photo on Match.com one evening after she had a fight with her boyfriend, just as a way of being spiteful. Martin is a 38-year-old entrepreneur from New York City who has also posted his profile on Match.com and has seen several women he would love to go out with. But his business is struggling, cash is tight and he would rather not part with the $24.99 subscriber fee. Instead, when he sees a woman he would like to contact, he gets friends who already subscribe to Match to email the woman for him and send along his contact information. No saying whether the women get turned off by this first impression of a cheap guy, but his story suggests how easy it is for people to abuse the system—in effect, to steal intellectual property. Jill, Caroline and Martin, in fact, all count as Match.com "members," but not as paying subscribers. The reservations they have about joining help show why most dating sites have far more members than paying subscribers. Match.com's 2002 ratio of 725,000 paying subscribers to eight million members is fairly typical of the entire industry. "We still have a lot of tire kickers," explains Todd Nelson, marketing director for gay dating site Gay11.com. "About 8 to 10 percent of our members are paying members. I would like to raise that."

To really understand the potential and the challenges that lie ahead for the online dating business, you have to go beyond the big cities and look at the places in Middle America, where trends are slower to stick. Oklahoma City, located pretty much smack in the middle of the country, thousands of miles from the technology centers on the West Coast and the media centers on the East Coast, is a good case study. The land is flat in Oklahoma City, the sky looms large and often there is a still silence in the air, reflecting the utter lack of any hustle and bustle. The people here are among the friendliest in America, but with big broad smiles they will tell tourists that there is really nothing in town worth seeing, that life here is a little bit boring. In recent years the city has built up a downtown entertainment and dining district that extends for several blocks, providing nightlife and street life and boat rides in a manmade canal, but this social center sits like a tiny oasis within the stillness. Locals say that new faces are hard to come by and young people in particular made regular road trips to Dallas three hours away just to break out of their familiar confines. The sense of confinement also produces many young marriages, however the National Center for Health Statistics says the divorce rate in Oklahoma is higher than any other state in the United States, except Arkansas and Nevada.

By many measures Oklahoma City would be ripe territory for Internet dating and, in fact, it is, particularly considering the relative lack of technological sophistication. Unlike the population of some larger metropolitan areas, many people in Oklahoma do not own computers, and they do not believe they are in the Dark Ages because of this. But among those people who are online, there is a rich narrative of Internet romance, from marriages forged between local college students to marriages betrayed through virtual relationships. All around town, the stories are everywhere. Rick, a 26-year-old aspiring musician, is engaged to a woman he met through the Internet. Andrew, a 22-year-old waiter, found something else: a long-distance relationship with a Florida woman, who revealed only after several meetings that she was married. "She would come visit about once a month, and she would always tell me about this guy who was her roommate, who was gay, and who just happened to have the same last name," Andrew recalled bitterly.

Personally, Andrew is skeptical about going back to the Internet to find a date, but all around him, everyone is doing it. The chef in the restaurant where he works is a 35-year-old divorced woman who has been corresponding with a man in Florida, mulling over whether to take him up on an invitation to visit. And, Andrew says, every last one of his single friends in town is looking for love or friendship online. Yet none of these people had joined, or even visited, an online dating service. They all used Internet chat rooms, where they found that regardless of what the topic of discussion was supposed to be, it always seemed to turn to matters of the heart. And it was free.

4

Love Minus Chemistry Equals Friendship

"I am not looking for a 'friend' or a 'friend with benefits' so if that's what you're looking for, then just pass me up. Cause I don't need any more immature guys in my life."

—A 19-year-old Iowa woman

The problem with so many dating services, says Dr. Neil Clark Warren, is that there is no proof that people who golf are more likely to fall in love with fellow golfers, or that a taste for quiet evenings by the fireplace reveals anything at all about one's character. People's income level and their political beliefs have surprisingly little to do with their ability to get along with their mates. Other things that you can't always screen for online, such as mental and emotional health, are critical. No one, moreover, has ever figured out the mystery at the heart of it all, or what creates chemistry, and while they go about pursuing that elusive state, they seem to fool themselves into believing that the process of selecting a spouse can be a relatively simple matter of lining up along similar superficial interests—and a mutual physical attraction. Don't even get him started on looks. "Like a new car that dramatically depreciates in value as soon as it is driven off the lot, physical appearance goes down in value far more rapidly than you might expect," says Warren.

A psychologist who has written a small library of books on the topic, Warren is full of aphorisms about that quest to find a life partner. No marriage can be stronger than the emotional health of the least healthy person, he insists. You will never get much more in a mate than you have to offer. In a society where more than 50 percent of marriages end in divorce, it is impossible to be too picky. And yes, hard as it may be to hear, love minus chemistry equals nothing more than a good friendship. Warren believes that the vast databases of people provided by most online dating sites are lost on a population of singles who have not been educated in the ways of finding a soul mate. They mistakenly scan for a pretty face, similar athletic tastes, a large income and other qualities that are relatively trivial in the scheme of things.

Marriage is hard enough when you have the right mate. Warren is convinced that the high divorce rate in the United States today is not so much due to people falling out of love, or succumbing to life's trials, as it is their failure to pick the proper partner in the first place. You will never hear Warren tell someone they could do worse, that out of all of those thousands of people who have posted their faces on the Internet, they should surely be able to find somebody to love. "I encourage people to figure out the kind of person they need to be really happy, and then to hold on to this set of criteria to the very end," he says. "Mismatchedness will always win out over hard work."

Warren's advice to people looking for love is to find out as much about both themselves and their potential partners as they can, and then let go and see if the chemistry exists. While he admits to being a terrible matchmaker on his own, he does believe he can help couples by providing the right questions for them to consider.

Warren is a bit of an enigma. Part moralistic churchgoer, he says sexual chemistry is essential to a good relationship, but advises it not be fully explored before marriage. Part mad scientist, he believes that physical attraction is created by thousands of subtle clues that people send out through their scents, their voices and their mannerisms, and that one day everyone will have their own personal blueprint of attraction that will make it quite simple to locate a soul mate, perhaps even through a computer search engine. "I don't believe in intuition," he explains. "I do believe that some people are extremely bright and attend to clues." He must include himself in this category of exceptionally bright people, because he found his wife, of 43 years, long before he had gained any insights about what it took to have a solid relationship. Today, he cites his enduring marriage as a professional accomplishment that qualifies him for the matchmaking business as much as all his years as a clinical psychologist. "We were blessed to have chosen each other when we lacked any comprehension of why we were doing so," he says. "We realize now that our marital success was based largely on luck, not good decision-making."

Like the man himself, Warren's vision is an odd hybrid of old-fashioned matchmaking and modern technology, a balance of deep introspection and advanced data processing. Where the Internet can be useful, Warren believes, is in processing all the information about character, values and little personality quirks, while providing a substantial list of people to search through. When you are as picky as Warren says you ought to be, you are going to have to start with a big pool of potential mates.

Eharmony.com, the Internet dating site Warren built and oversees today, has a little more than half a million members, which makes it relatively small compared to some industry leaders. Then again, it probably has a smaller target audience. Gays or lesbians are not welcomed at eHarmony; Warren says he just doesn't understand enough about homosexual attraction. And the lengthy eHarmony registration process will almost certainly weed out people looking only for a one-night stand. However, eHarmony.com is part of a growing movement to incorporate sophisticated psychological profiling into online dating in an attempt to make the process of finding lasting love less random.

It might sound a lot like those old computer dating services from 40 years ago until you look at some of the information that eHarmony collects from its singles. "True or false," asks one question on the psychological profile that members are required to complete before joining, "I always read all the warning literature on side effects before taking any medication." Although the site does allow members to describe their physical appearance and post photos, the emphasis lies elsewhere. Everyone who joins eHarmony receives Warren's book, *Date or Soul Mate: How to Know If Someone Is Worth Pursuing in Two Dates or Less*, which prods them to get beyond that trap of listing the same qualities and activities that just about everyone in the world wants. (Sense of humor, romantic walks on the beach, someone who is capable of being both serious and silly, someone who is as comfortable in a tuxedo/little black dress as they are in three days of stubble/jeans and a ponytail). Warren's book provides a list of 50 "must-haves" and 50 "can't-stands" for people to ponder. Most people, he reasons, understand the importance of things like sense of humor and kindness. Those qualities consistently rank in the top ten traits singles report as being essential in their spouse. On the other hand, they might not have thought about other issues that surface later in a relationship. Things like autonomy or finding someone who will give them some personal space. Or parent care—a spouse who will accept the responsibility of caring for aged parents when that time comes. Such factors, says Warren, may be equally or more critical in determining whether a couple will be able to stay together until death.

Likewise, traits that are generally considered deal breakers, such as excessive vanity, dishonesty and cheating, all rank high on the most common "can't stand" lists. But fewer people think to screen for other potentially undesirable traits such as a tendency to gossip, a gambling addiction or an exceedingly flirtatious nature. Although similar levels of energy, levels of ambition, personal habits and views about spirituality mean a lot, one of the most interesting things his research has turned up, Warren says, is that money, in and of itself, rarely is the cause of a failed marriage. He does believe, however, that persistent money troubles may likely be the result of a serious psychological flaw, which can easily ruin a relationship. Because of this conviction that emotional health is critical to a lasting partnership, the eHarmony test seeks to weed out people who are habitual liars, or those who suffer from addictions, extreme neuroses and other character disorders. People who appear mentally unstable will not find any potential matches on eHarmony, not even with other unstable types. Unlike the founders of TheraDate, Warren does not think that two neurotics cancel each other out. And unlike some other online dating services that suggest that anyone can find a match, eHarmony is proud of the fact that it deems as many as 20 percent of all its applicants unmatchable.

The company makes a big outreach between Thanksgiving and Valentine's Day, a period it says can be a long and lonely stretch for single people. It was at the start of that holiday cluster that Julie Fitzpatrick, a 28-year-old makeup artist and bartender living outside of Philadelphia, became interested in the service. Conventional wisdom holds that people under 30 who grew up with the Internet are more likely to be comfortable using Internet dating services, but in truth, many young people have never entertained such a move. Fitzpatrick said that neither she nor any of her close single friends used the Internet to socialize. She, for one, did not believe it was at all possible to feel chemistry through a computer. An upbeat and chatty woman who talks easily about personal things like falling in love and dates from hell, she was drawn to eHarmony mainly because its extensive psychological profile intrigued her. She devoted a full two hours to providing thoughtful answers to all its questions. How comfortable would she feel if her spouse were to become involved in one of the following kinds of interactions with a member of the opposite sex: Flirting? Slow Dancing? Kissing on the lips? On a scale of one to seven how impulsive was she? How neat? Uncomplicated? Persistent? Aggressive? Jealous? Outspoken? Stubborn? Other than her appearance, what was the first thing that people noticed about her? What was something that people did not notice about her that she wished they would? Did she ever feel plotted against?

Fitzpatrick went into eHarmony with a far less scientific approach to life and love. "I believe that if you want to make God laugh, you make a plan," she said. At 28, she had already suffered multiple heartbreaks, including the premature death of her mother, and at age 22, the end of an intense eight-year relationship with her high school boyfriend. But after investing so much time to complete the eHarmony application, she began reflecting that her social life did have room for improvement. Fitzpatrick had not had a serious boyfriend for five years and recently had been spending most of her time with her father, her grandmother, a newborn niece, gay men friends who each Monday dragged her off to "Drag Night," and assorted married friends. She followed through and joined eHarmony partly out of curiosity and partly because of the time already invested. Among her own personal "can't stands," Fitzpatrick listed cheating, an inability to accept blame, and a judgmental character who found fault with everyone. Her "must haves" included a sharp wit and ability to handle life's frustrations with patience, and a mature and experienced sexual partner. "I'm 28 years old, let's be real," she said. When she posed for a photo to post on the site, she was careful to show a generous amount of cleavage.

Shortly after she fed all that information into the system, it came back with a lengthy analysis of her character. There was the obvious "You have to be with people," and the more insightful

"You have a high trust level of others and occasionally you may have trusted too much." A few of the computer-generated observations she even found to be uncanny. "One will generally know how you are feeling, whether good or bad, because you let others know your moods easily." The service also provided a list of qualities Fitzpatrick wanted in a mate. It suggested she would like, among other things, someone who moved casually and informally, someone who was prepared to listen to many stories, someone who planned sufficient time to talk and listen, along with a relationship that would play out in "a predictable environment with few surprises."

She had to admit it was pretty accurate, but Fitzpatrick quickly became chagrined to discover that all that time invested, all those insights provided did not grant her the freedom to contact all the men on eHarmony. Instead, she got a much shorter list of potential matches, only those who fit the age range and psychological characteristics that eHarmony had deemed acceptable. Singles interested in following Warren's theories of dating must accept his entire philosophy. He does not believe in big age gaps between partners and argues that plain people should not pursue lookers, because even if they succeed, they will spend their entire married life worried about being left.

It was really only a handful of men that eHarmony deemed appropriate for Julie Fitzpatrick. And then, it was extremely slow going. Because she did not work in an office and have access to email all day long, she was only able to spend time on the eHarmony site every few days, when her roommate was not monopolizing the computer. So much for finding a date for the holidays. Thanksgiving had come and gone, Christmas was not far away and she had still not had so much as a direct email exchange with any of her potential matches. Before she could email any men, talk to them on the phone or even see their photos, the paternalistic eHarmony required that she do a little more probing of character. It instructed her, once she had located a man who sounded interesting, to select some questions from the psychological test and request to see the answers he had supplied.

Fitzpatrick loved all this analytical stuff. The problem was that not everyone else on eHarmony was so committed. One man had shown some potential until she read his response to the question, "Other than your parents, who has been the most influential person in your life?" His answer: "I'd have to think about that." Fitzpatrick did not know whether to be amused or exasperated. "Couldn't he have thought about it a little more and then given an answer?" she retorted.

Although singles themselves are not always attuned to their inner psychological workings, many businesses believe this is the real service to the dating industry the Internet can provide. "The functionality of Yahoo and Match.com, other than their newer instant messaging capabilities, has not changed since 1995," argues James Currier, the founder of eMode.com, another Web site that offers a dating service based on psychological profiling. Unlike both the straightforward age-height-weight-hobbies approach of sites like Match.com, and the painstakingly slow approach taken by eHarmony, eMode is pop psychology at its finest. The company offers a multitude of quick and entertaining tests such as the Emotional IQ Test, the Career Personality Test, the What Zodiac Sign Should You Be? and What Breed of Dog Are You? tests.

"Our number-one interest is ourselves," says Currier, who discovered that if he were a dog, his people-loving nature would make him a golden retriever, according to one of the psych-lite tests featured on his site. Currier's site grew out of his interest in technology and people. After graduating from business school in the late 1990s, Currier said he saw that a lot of people were taking the Myers-Briggs Corporate Personality Test, but was surprised to find that the test was still being circulated in mostly paper form. "It occurred to me that the Internet would transform it, make it instant and colorful, allow you to share, without having to get everyone together in one room."

In 2001, two years after eMode was launched as a general sort of fun self-discovery destination, the company decided to add a dating feature based on the premise, not unlike that of eHarmony, that attraction does not mean compatibility. "You can find hot people in the nude online all day long. That is not the issue," said Currier, who remembers the dating marathon leading up to meeting his future wife was one full of superficial attractions that looked good from a distance but held no substance. Currier's own theory of love is one of physical chemistry and shared values. Hobbies and interests, like a love of golf, he maintains, are conversation starters more than anything else. "Superficial interests are not that important," he argues. "They don't have to be the same. It's good to have diversity in a relationship."

The eMode registration process is a lot less onerous than eHarmony's, but it still manages to collect some serious character details. Questions range from which flowers make the best romantic gift, to one's philosophy about sex and preferred breakup tactic (serious discussion versus not returning phone calls). It takes almost no time to complete, but eMode says its questions do prove useful in cracking the compatibility puzzle. As eMode rapidly approaches one million registered members, it expects to refine its matching technology so that it can conduct more in-depth analyses and make better links between personality and compatibility. "Right now, we have 3.2 billion questions answered in our database. It's going to start to get really interesting." At its most ambitious level, eMode, says Currier, is in the business of "making tangible a host of human intangibles," another way of saying that, with enough information, there might really be a way to get at the scientific basis for chemistry.

5

NEEDLE IN A HAYSTACK

"I am a reasonably happy but lonely widow looking for companionship and possibly more. I do not look my age and try not to act it. I am happy to spend quiet time at home, but would love to have someone to snuggle with."

—A 78-year-old Texas woman

In 1984, after years of living estranged from each other under the same roof, Florence and her husband parted ways, effectively ending a marriage that had always been starved of affection. Florence had once been a boy-crazy teenager, falling in and out of love all the time, before she gave into family pressures to break an engagement with the man she thought was Mr. Right to marry a Mr. Not Right At All. As a separated middle-aged woman, Florence emerged into a world where it seemed there were zero available men. Not overly eager to date, she was nonetheless taken back by the lack of opportunity, and after several years on her own, became resigned to living the rest of her life that way. When she joined an online dating service at 70, she had been divorced for 18 years and had not been out with a man in as long. So the amount of interest she received on the Internet almost instantly seemed too good to be true.

One of the dating services Florence joined provided up-to-the-minute data on how many people were reading her profile. During Florence's first month online, some 31 people—she presumed most of them single men—had looked at it. Florence did not know any single men, never mind 31 of them, but there they were. Each had stopped to read about the self-described "active and attractive lady" who loved her dog, traveled frequently—and smoked often. That was a man a day. Eighteen years without any and now she was attracting potential suitors at a rate of one a day. How could she complain? What Florence did not know was that Annabel, the divorced mother 30 years her junior, had drawn 710 people to her profile in the same timeframe. Annabel was more than 20 times as popular as Florence. While Florence's email box sat for weeks filled a sorry one percent of capacity, Annabel's was maxed out. The email provider was trying to sell her extra storage space.

If dating is really just a numbers game, one of the first things people learn when they go online is that the old numbers do not apply. You might be hearing from ten interested suitors every day, but that does not necessarily mean much. Someone else out there is getting ten times as much mail. Dating on the Internet means dating on Internet time, finding as many prospects in a month as you might have otherwise located in a lifetime and, for some people, discovering that none of them are right. Sure, there are the stories of people who fell in love, married, and had triplets with the first person they ever met, but many others have searched for years without finding what they wanted. There are volumes of people to choose from, on the largest Internet dating sites, more profiles than you could ever screen in a systematic fashion, and this creates its own set of problems. For the people in the most sought-after demographic categories, usually young women, the challenge often is just to find time to read through all the mail received. Maybe her soul mate was the 80th person to write to her, but she never got around to reading his note, because she got tied up on the first 20 letters she received. For the men, who typically find themselves doing the pursuing online, there is a different challenge. Most can easily identify 100 promising women and contact them all, only to be stung when not a single one writes back. On the Internet, the numbers can throw you.

Or they can baffle you. Angelo DiMeglio was baffled. The rugged-yet-gentle-looking 45-year-old construction worker who lived year-round on the island of Martha's Vineyard, off the coast of Massachusetts, was not so much interested in how many women stopped to look at his picture as he was perturbed by the lack of follow-through. Late that summer, while buying some wintertime gear on a factory outlet shopping trip to Maine, DiMeglio's friends had reminded him that there was one thing he would really enjoy during the long winter on the island that most people left after Labor Day. They thought an online dating service might be a good way for him to find a warm body, so right then and there, they all went into a cyber café and signed him up. Seven weeks later, although the computer told DiMeglio that 340 people had seen his profile—he presumed most of them single women—not a single person had written to him. Here was a nice-looking guy, who was easy to talk to, had steady work and was so handy around the house that he had actually built his own house, and all these women who supposedly were looking for those very qualities were passing him over. He became more proactive and started initiating conversations with women who lived close to the island, but they all ignored him too. No short notes just to say "hi." No noncommittal invitations for coffee. Nada. At the rate Angelo was going, he would be lucky to have a casual pen pal by the spring, let alone a girlfriend. "I think this service sucks!" he said one chilly November weekend, shortly after he had spent Thanksgiving alone. "You would think that at least one chick would say, 'Look at this guy, I think I'll send him a message.' I can't quite figure it out."

The dating pickings have always gotten slimmer as people aged or settled in out-of-the-way places, and although the Internet can in theory fix that, in practice it does not always work that way. Seniors get asked out much less than 20-year-olds, just like in the real world, and high-speed modems can't keep you warm at night when you live on an island accessible only by boat or plane. Noah is an 84-year-old retired air force officer in Florida who went online a couple of years after his wife died and discovered hundreds of single and computer-literate women in their seventies. Most of them rejected him, even though his active schedule of camping and hiking, biking, fishing and boating left him more fit than they were. "When they found out I was 84, they said that I was too old but they wanted to remain friends," he said. Florence, meanwhile, had a hard time even getting to the point of platonic friendship. After two months online, she had still not heard from a single man.

What the Internet can do is help people cast a wider net to locate however many sympathetic individuals are out there. On some of the most advanced dating sites, DiMeglio could have searched any number of random terms, like "island life" or "middle of the woods," and found a handful of women who had also sacrificed the stimulation of a city to live in natural, isolated beauty. Maybe one of them would have been more willing to travel to meet him. He could have searched the term "woodworking" to find women who shared his hobbies. But that would still pale in comparison to the embarrassment of riches awaiting a 25-year-old male living in New York City, who on the biggest online dating sites can usually find at least 100 single women his exact same age living within five miles of his doorstep. The irony, of course, is that in a densely populated city rich in street life like New York, an outgoing 25-year-old could probably meet at least that many women offline in the real world, that old-fashioned social forum that hard-core Internet daters have started referring to as "the wild." So, even though it offers limited benefits for people who are already outside the mainstream, Internet dating has become an especially valuable tool for people living on the margins of society: seniors, disabled people, small-town people and people who feel strongly about marrying within their own religion.

Peter Storandt is neither elderly nor island-bound, but he was old enough and isolated enough that when he found himself single again, it seemed time to try something new. At 56, he was working as a recruiter for an Oklahoma City law school, and his job frequently kept him on the road and out of the local social scene. Widowed once after 11 years of marriage, Storandt had recently divorced his second wife of 16 years. He was drawn to the small SinglesWithScruples site because it seemed to value character over income, and it asked some probing, character-revealing questions. In places, the SinglesWithScruples registration form resembles a college application, asking members to list "a person I admire, and why," as well as a prized possession, a cherished belief, and "a significant event in my life, other than divorce or children." After he signed up, Storandt discovered some other benefits of the Internet. It helped him to bring his social life along when he went on the road. One of the first connections he made was with a woman living more than a thousand miles away in Michigan, and he arranged to meet her for dinner while he was in town on business. The attraction was strong, but Storandt ultimately voted against the distance and went back online to look for someone closer to home. Despite his intentions, distance seemed to disappear over email once again, and Storandt found himself getting closer and closer to a woman from Virginia. Again, he put aside his concerns and arranged to meet his latest long-distance friend. They settled on an independent location in Texas.

In the meantime, however, Storandt had started corresponding with a third woman, who lived right near him in Oklahoma City. On the eve of his trip to meet the Virginia woman, the Oklahoma woman made a strong case for the benefits of a local relationship and stepped up the pressure that they meet. Remembering how things had gone with the Michigan woman, Storandt knew she had a point. He met the Oklahoma woman and the chemistry was instant. He made a last-minute phone call to the Virginia woman, telling her not to come to Texas. Storandt, who recently celebrated his first wedding anniversary to Judy, from Oklahoma, said the Virginia woman was gracious about his change of heart. When he spoke to her again some time later, she told him she was corresponding with a man from Australia.

By the time Judy met Peter Storandt, she had been dabbling in online dating for a couple of years and had started to feel like a relationship expert. She had even drafted a book about looking for love on the Internet, offering tips on what to wear for that first offline meeting (comfortable shoes that won't distract you from the conversation) and how to read the subtext of an email correspondence. Judy had learned by trial and error all sorts of things she did not want in a spouse, and she was convinced that people's undesirable qualities came through in subtle and not-so-subtle comments and gestures. Guys who said that they liked "romantic evenings in front of the fireplace," she said, "were guys who were very possessive and needed a lot of your time." On the other hand, she worried that many men who said they liked "a romantic evening out with a good bottle of wine" could be alcoholics. Call her suspicious, but Judy's love life had not run a smooth course. So, one night when she went out with a nice recovering alcoholic who had managed to stay on the wagon for years, she detected a different kind of red flag. "He had clearly traded in his alcohol addiction for a food addiction," she said. "All he talked about all night was food and how much he loved to eat. He was a standup kind of a guy, but I was not comfortable with the role that food played in his life."

As Judy Storandt tells it, the Internet finally led her to her own needle in a haystack, which is about how challenging it had seemed for a once-widowed and twice-divorced, religious and well-traveled professional woman living in Oklahoma to locate a suitable mate. "There are an amazing number of men here who have never left the state," she said. Judy grew up in Wisconsin and had lived in Indiana and Louisiana before moving to Oklahoma, along the way putting herself through law school while also being a single mother of three boys. Peter, her fourth husband, had lived in at least half the major cities in the country, from San Francisco to Miami. Along with sharing the experiences of an early death of a first spouse and

Oklahoma City residents Peter and Judy Storandt lived in the same neighborhood but found each other online. Reuters.

the failure of subsequent marriages, the nature of their life's disappointments was in many ways parallel. You would not necessarily know it from their spotty marriage records, but they were both churchgoers with traditional values. Each had at one point in their lives specifically looked for a spouse in a religious setting, figuring that would be a no-fault foundation for a solid relationship—only to have those ensuing marriages fail. Peter had fallen for the soprano soloist in his church choir, and Judy had married a fellow parishioner. "I had thought, I am so lucky. I met this great man at church. He will never leave me," she said of her third husband, who later did leave her.

Online dating has given new meaning to the term "church social," or, as the case may be "temple social," and is being embraced especially by members of smaller or more localized religions. Meeting a Mormon in and around the church's world headquarters in Salt Lake City, Utah, may be relatively easy, but it becomes more challenging the farther one moves away. Keeping a strong sense of community has become more difficult as the ranks of the faithful have dispersed. Today the church has 60,000 missionaries fanned out around the world, and only 14 percent of its 11 million members reside in Utah. Besides, even in Salt Lake, many serious Mormons say the church social and youth volunteer group scene is getting old. In 2001, a group of Mormons produced the comedy film *The Singles Ward* to dramatize the plight of a group of religious singles in a modern world. They poked fun at their faith with the tagline "the road to eternal marriage has never been longer." Mormons are not required to marry other Mormons, but the religion places a particularly strong emphasis on the belief that the spouse you chose in this lifetime stays with you for eternity, so most try to stick within the faith.

Several years ago, Utah software engineer Bob Haupt had a vision for an online dating service for fellow Mormons. In 1996, Haupt founded LDSSingles.com, named for the Mormon Church of Latter Day Saints. Because of the Mormon congregation's scattered nature, many of the site's success stories are long-distance romances.

Catholics may have an easier time than Mormons do finding people of their own faith to date, but Victor, a 28-year-old Ph.D. candidate, found it almost impossible when he went to school in Fargo, North Dakota, a city of about 90,000. Right in the middle of a sprawling university campus, the setting that was supposed to be the best in the world for finding love and sex, Victor was dismayed to find that the overwhelming majority of students were Lutheran. He said that in Fargo, a stigma and a taint of desperation are still associated with the Internet, and he never would have used it himself had he not been a hard-core Catholic living in a Protestant world. Another Christian was not good enough for Victor; he had to have a Catholic. "Being a practicing Catholic," he wrote on his Internet profile, "I know that things would not work out with someone who is not Catholic, or has no interest in being Catholic. As far as divorces go, if you are divorced you are off limits to me unless you had an annulment. I probably sound like a jerk, but I should just state right now, that if you don't fit this preliminary profile, it won't go beyond the friendship stage." Victor may have thought he had a novel idea, departing from the usual college parties and getting down to business online, but he actually was not all that original. At the time he posted his profile, there were a few hundred Fargo men between the ages of 20 and 30 on some of the largest online dating sites, all saying they were either tired of small-town life, tired of the bar scene, tired of having to go out in the cold to meet women or just tired of all the Lutherans.

One specialized site that has had particular success is JDate.com, part of the MatchNet network of dating sites, which has helped Jews from Los Angeles to Jerusalem find Jewish partners. In cities like New York, the term JDate has come to be regarded as an obvious place for unattached Jews to look for mates. Self-described nice Jewish boys Michael Mandelberg and his brother Josh both found their future wives on JDate within months of each other, shortly after they had finished school and returned to their native Los Angeles. Michael, a 25-year-old who works in marketing, said he first learned about the site from his older brother when he was in medical school in San Francisco, where he was not meeting a lot of nice Jewish girls. While Josh ultimately met and became engaged to a woman who had attended his same high school, Michael met a girl who was still in college but not enamored of the college social scene. "It wasn't easy for me because I was a little reserved," said Janice Mandelberg, a couple of months after her wedding to Michael. "You are surrounded by so many different people. I think that intimidated me a lot." The Mandelbergs also have a younger brother still in college, and they sometimes joke that they will be three-for-three if he also marries someone from JDate.

JDate also serves a purpose similar to that of LDSSingles: providing a critical social outlet for those living in places where the Jewish population is thin. When Dina Tanners discovered JDate, she was a 52-year-old divorcee who, in the eight years since she had split from her husband, had found few men to date in her hometown of Spokane, Washington. Although Tanners eventually became another JDate success story, it was not an easy or pain-free process for her. First, there was the application, which took her six weeks to fill out. Like so many other people who toy with the idea of online dating but can never seem to follow through, Tanners did not know what to say about herself. The JDate registration form includes many questions that require thought—some people even call them essay questions—such as a description of an ideal first date. Tanners had not been on a date in 25 years and was stumped. Then there was the hard truth that being a woman in her fifties, she did not have an abundance of men writing to her. When she finally worked up the nerve to reply to one man from Seattle, and then to take the extra leap of phoning him while on a trip there to visit her mother, Tanners was sorely disappointed. He never returned the call.

Yet Tanners was resilient, and when she heard from her second JDate suitor, she had a good feeling right away. He sent her a photo of himself wearing a sweatshirt that said, "Too Many Books, Not Enough Time," and a yarmulke. She found both the suggestion of intellect and the strong Jewish identity appealing. In an early correspondence, he explained that while he was not an Orthodox Jew, he wore the yarmulke to show the world that he was not in any way ashamed of his identity. There had been an uncomfortable incident during the Gulf War of 1991 when a coworker had suggested that he hide the fact that he was Jewish. Instead, he had chosen to advertise it. "That fit in very strongly with my own Jewish identity," Tanners said. The next time she traveled the 300 miles to visit her mother in Seattle, she had better luck on the social front.

Howard Cockerham followed through with his plans to meet her and showed up in the same attire as in his photo. They stayed out talking until two in the morning. "I woke up my Mom and said, 'I met the nicest guy!' I had never done that in high school." Tanners, who eventually married Howard, had a strong offline, even old-fashioned, component to her courtship from the start. After she had met Howard in Seattle, but before she invited him to come and visit her, she contacted her local rabbi to quiz him on the Jewish community in Cockerham's hometown, Bellingham, Washington. He contacted the Bellingham synagogue, and it was not until she received a favorable report that she decided to go ahead with the visit.

JDate lets singles further narrow their search by asking members to identify their ethnicity, say whether they keep kosher, whether and how often they go to synagogue, and what branch of Judaism—orthodox, conservative, Hasidic, reform or traditional—they identify with. About 7 percent of those who join check another box labeled "unaffiliated." It does not necessarily mean that the person joining is Christian or of some other non-Jewish faith, but it might. Unlike LDSSingles, which is open only to members of the Mormon faith, JDate allows non-Jews to join, asking only that they be honest about their religion. This open-door policy has spawned another curious subgroup of people on its site: non-Jews looking for Jews. Although some JDate members take offense at non-Jews joining, others are amused. "I think that stereotypes play a part in this," said Jeremy, a Jewish JDate member from southern California. "For example, the idea that Jewish men are nice, nurturing, smart, funny, and look like Seinfeld... I'm kidding about the Seinfeld part." In all seriousness, Jeremy said he occasionally hears from Christian women seeking Jewish men, some who seem convinced that Jewish men are more romantic. Bill, a Christian from San Jose, California, said he was having a field day on JDate for exactly the opposite reason. "I've found that most Jewish women would rather not date a Jewish man," he said.

Marco Sorani always knew that at some point in the future he would want to end his life of casual dating and settle down with the right woman. That change from frivolous to focused came sooner than he expected, however, when in 1994, at the age of 25, he was paralyzed in a swimming accident. It was not that Sorani's romantic life died after the accident; he dated his physical therapist, and later kept up a busy social calendar of parties, blind dates and visits to bars with friends. He remained outgoing and optimistic, convinced that his using a wheelchair would either not be an issue to women, or be a minor one that could be overcome. Still, he was somewhat apprehensive about first impressions. It was partly that apprehension, and partly just the regular challenges of being a busy professional whose other single friends were rapidly pairing off, that led him to join Match.com when he was 30. A San Francisco resident, Sorani had noticed a Match.com billboard one day while driving to his Silicon Valley office. When Sorani registered on Match.com, he came across a box where he could check "disabled" under body type. He chose not to, though, preferring to get an email rapport going first. One of the first times he arranged to meet a woman offline, he told her over the phone that he was in a wheelchair, and she laughed.

"She said, 'No way!'" Sorani recalled. "'The last guy I met from Match.com was in a chair too.'"

Sorani did not end up pursuing a relationship with that woman, but the nonchalance and humor with which she had responded to his disability had put him at ease. Siobhan Fleming, the woman who later became his wife, also proved to be quite accepting from the start. "It was a little bit of a shock when he told me," she said. "I wasn't really sure, but I felt that I wanted to meet him anyway." Siobhan and Marco said they felt comfortable together right away, but their relationship did not immediately take off. There were other things getting in the way, mainly all the other people from Match.com. When they met, in fact, Siobhan and Marco were both casually dating other people they had met online. It was that same challenge so many online daters face, of having to wade through volumes of people. Siobhan in

Marco and Siobhan Sorani were both overwhelmed by all the options online, but quickly settled on each other. Reuters.

particular had been inundated with mail. She never had the opportunity to actually read through the profiles of men on the site because emails from about 12 different men were landing in her box each day. It was all she could do to respond to that mail. "I felt like dating had become a part-time job," she said. "I actually took notes, because I couldn't keep all of them straight." But by the time it got down to Marco and one other man, she said the choice was easy. "The more I saw Marco, the more I started to think how boring the other guy was. He started to really annoy me." If dating two or more people at once used to be frowned upon, it is common, perhaps inevitable, among many people belonging to sites like Match.com. As Siobhan saw it,

there were benefits of juggling, like being able to compare and contrast, and hurry the decision-making process along.

For all his insistence that the women he dated be open-minded,
Marco himself remained a little stubborn on one point. He did not
want Siobhan telling his friends and family members the truth
about how they had met. Like so many other people who pride
themselves on being open about their sex lives, their finances and
political beliefs, Marco was secretive about using an online dating
service. Things got confusing because Siobhan had always told her
friends the truth. When she started spending more time with
Marco's friends, she said, she had to remember to switch to a
made-up story about an introduction through a mutual friend. "It
was something vague and unverifiable," she remembers. In early
2003, a couple of months after they were married, Marco agreed to
go public with the true story of how they met.

One reason seniors like Florence and Noah did not immediately have as much luck as people in other specialized segments of
the population is that even among seniors who are single and
healthy and interested in dating, Internet proficiency remains low,
and old-fashioned social networks are often quite strong. Jerrold
Kemp, who wrote the book *Older Couples, New Couplings* in
2000 after he fell in love and married for the second time at the age
of 75, said seniors still rely largely on offline networks, such as
square dancing, bird watching or church groups, far more than
they use the computer. "I think seniors are not, proportionately
speaking, using computers as much as other people," he said. A
few of the couples Kemp featured in his book had met, as seniors,
through newspaper personals, but more had connected at church
or retirement communities, or had been longstanding friends who
turned to each other for company only after their spouses had died.

But what is a strong-willed seventy-something woman who
does not fit the mold of little old church lady to do? For Emma, the
alternative was to find an online chat room for atheists, a place she
went to often, when the offline world started to feel oppressively

Christian. Divorced since the age of 49, Emma had lived well into her sixties without ever meeting anyone with whom she wished to pursue a serious relationship. Nor did she have romance on her mind when she connected with William in an online discussion group about atheism that she found on a Web site for seniors. But it was easy to build an online friendship with someone who shared her passion for rational thought. For six years Emma and William kept each other company over email, until at some point it seemed only natural to exchange photos. After they did, William decided to set out on a 2,000-mile journey from his home in southern Indiana to the coastal town in Oregon where Emma lived. It was not a simple direct flight, but one with many bus and taxicab connections on both ends, and when he finally arrived, it was hardly love at first sight. William was worn out from his travels, and Emma said, he looked it. Yet she has shared their story several times, with friends and in online forums to discuss romance in the golden years, and each time she does, she is careful to include the detail that they were lovers by day two. Today, in addition to having a live-in boyfriend, Emma is an outspoken advocate of online correspondence among seniors, even if they prefer to talk about, God forbid, religion. "There are people who are so lonely there is no telling what they would do without the Internet," she said. "After 25 years of being fussy, it's nice to find someone who is 95 percent acceptable."

Like Emma, many Internet-literate seniors lack the confidence or conviction to join an online dating service, but often connect more casually through chat rooms. Those who have formed relationships online often say it is slow going and that the process of dating online at their age is fraught with its own set of problems. Women who may have been wined, dined and aggressively pursued by their first husbands often discover this time around that building a relationship is all their responsibility. There is a kind of role reversal for people over 60 online, in which the women actively initiate conversations, while men as old as 75 find themselves in the enviable position of sitting back and eliminating the undesirables. One man who met his second wife online when he was 64 said he rejected several other women from all over the United States, Canada and even New Zealand. He said many were simply looking for people to travel with them on expensive tour packages and seemed to assume he would foot the bill.

As her email box remained empty day after day, Florence began to understand as much. If she wanted to meet someone she would probably have to do the heavy lifting. So, when several weeks had passed without her receiving a single note, she gingerly set out to contact a few men. At first the selection seemed abundant. There was the "68-year-old fun-loving guy in real good shape and health," the 70-year-old who said he enjoyed all people but wanted to find "the one to share life with in a committed relationship," the 68-year-old who was recently widowed after 27 years of marriage and was seeking a companion to "dance to the oldies" and join him on his daily three-mile walks. When she read beyond the head-lines, though, she had to eliminate many of them. Almost all of the men were non-smokers, and most of them had specifically stated their preference for another non-smoker. Others were, as they say, after just one thing. A 69-year-old who lived about 20 miles away said he wanted "an erotic pen pal to discuss sexual fantasies."

Finally, Florence saw a profile for one man who didn't sound like a sex maniac and said that he would be willing to meet a smoker, even though he did not smoke himself. She was as much of a stranger to email as she was to Internet dating, and she had not yet acquired that comfortable rambling style of teenagers and many office workers who spend an inordinate amount of time communicating electronically. She hardly knew what to say to this unknown man on the other end of the computer, but she managed to type off a couple of ice-breaking questions. Exactly what part of town did he live in? Did he happen to like dogs?

A couple of days later came the response. "I live in northeast Philadelphia. I am not a dog lover. Take care."

6

BURKAS AND VISAS

"I am currently living here even though the war is going on. I guess I must have an adventurous spirit. If you are in Kuwait, how about coffee at Starbucks?"

—A 51-year-old American woman living in Kuwait

About a month after September 11, 2001, when xenophobia was at a peak in the United States and racial profiling was being debated as sensible policy, a joke was widely circulated over email, poking fun at the sex lives of the Afghan people. "Taliban Singles Online," it read, and in place of the smiling faces and shapely bodies typically featured on American dating sites, it showed ten photos of women you could not see at all. They wore burkas that covered them from head to toe.

"Make me one of your wives," read the profile of one woman, who looked like a ghost behind a thick, white head covering. Like all of the fictitious ads on the page, this one listed the woman's occupation, hobbies and income all as "not permitted." Another photo

79

beckoned with the question "R U A Terrorist with a heart?" while a third offered the ironic description, "Not like all the other women." From what the picture showed, that woman was pretty much identical to the nine others, except that she wore a burka in a rather unusual shade of brown. It was probably just the timing, but even some very politically correct people found the joke very funny. Imagine a culture that demanded such extreme modesty from its female population ever allowing them to use the sex-saturated Internet to get a date. What was the point if you couldn't show your face anyway?

The Afghans, or at least some other conservative Muslim people, may have the last laugh. As a bunch of Westerners mocked another country's ways, there already existed a huge bazaar of Muslim and Arab singles on the Internet. Men and women from Saudi Arabia to Morocco have not only heard of this thing called Internet dating, but many are by now pretty adept at it. A 40-year-old executive manager in Kuwait posts an ad for "love and fun with a pretty lady"; a teenaged girl from Yemen improvises American pop culture with the verse "Show me the meaning of being lonely/Tell me why I can't be by your side." A 53-year-old divorcee from Dubai asks, "Can there be a soul mate in the middle of the desert?" And a 25-year-old Saudi advertises his wallet and his ego with this introduction, "Looks is something money can easily buy and I can prove it!!!" Forget face coverings; many traditional Muslim women take off their head scarves too and put on a little eye liner before posing for their online photos. A 39-year-old woman from Algeria recently posted a photo describing herself as "hot and heavy," with a taste for spandex and "forward men."

Dorri, a 32-year-old schoolteacher from Tehran, was moping over a lost boyfriend one afternoon when her teenage niece suggested she make herself busy on the Internet. Dorri did not have the money to afford her own computer, so she went to a cyber café, where her eyes were opened to a whole new subculture. Everyone, it seemed, was using the Internet for social purposes. "Most of the young people use it as a means to find new friends in other countries," she explained over email. "I know a lot of them who have found good friends in other countries." Dorri was not specifically looking for someone from another country, although she said that because of the poor economy at home, foreign men did have some appeal. The boyfriend she was trying to get over when she logged onto the Internet in the first place had broken up with her only because he did not think he had enough money to continue the relationship. "I could not believe him, but one day he invited some of my girlfriends and I to his home," she said. "They were very poor, and then I believed him." At the local cyber café, some of Dorri's peers were locating Americans who would send them CDs and books. Others were serious about finding a mate, and just within her close circle of friends was a woman who had connected with a man in Texas, arranged to meet him in Turkey, gotten engaged and was in the process of applying for a visa.

It would hardly be accurate, though, to present the Internet dating scene in Iran or other conservative Muslim countries as something people pursue only as a means to secure a visa, or even to import liberal Western ways back home. Just as in the United States, everyone in these countries has a different reason for going online, from finding a wealthy spouse to just killing time. Their motives also vary from country to country, depending on the relative restrictions under which people live. While some join American dating services, participation is much higher in local chat rooms that people can access for free, or on one of the growing number of Arab or Muslim-specific sites such as Arab2Love.com or Zawaj.com, a Muslim matrimonial site that seeks to connect religious Muslim men and women the world over, from New Zealand to Sudan. Typically, these sites are published in English, because it is considered the language people are most likely to have in common. Postings often appear in broken English, and those who post ads usually emphasize that they are seeking a religious spouse and are interested only in relationships that will lead to marriage. "I am looking for a sincere, honest husband, only Arabs," read one recent ad on Zawaj from a 36-year-old Iraqi woman. "Good hearted, and honest of his intentions for marriage, not waste my time with silly chat." An Arab man living in Ireland posted an ad for "a Muslim lady who is caring, good looking, pious."

Even those people who do join American dating sites seem to be motivated more by a nagging curiosity than a desire to immerse themselves in the ways of the West. Many who claim to yearn for a little sexual freedom often recoil when they discover the anything-goes attitude online. In Iran in particular, people who venture online seem to be testing the limits of a society where the rules have loosened just enough to make dating more confusing than ever. Unmarried men and women say they are not supposed to be alone together, but are getting away with it more and more. "Something has changed here, and yet it is illegal. Everything is hidden and so complicated to explain," Maheen, a 42-year-old accountant, also from Tehran, wrote in an email that grappled not only with the English language but the subtle undercurrents of change in a country where the fundamentalist regime had started to show its age. "There are a lot of women here who think and feel like American women." Still, Maheen was quickly turned off by her own online dating experience. "I met some men who are married and wanted just to have a girlfriend for sex, so I refused," she said. "I thought that maybe I would never find the right guy this way. I do chat with some people who show interest in me, but I cannot trust them after all. Eventually their way goes to a sexual relationship, which is just not in my thought."

Another class of Internet consumers in the Middle East has no need for an American spouse or a taste of Western living. Young Muslims from the wealthiest families and who were educated abroad complain that it is hard to readjust to the rules at home, and they find that the Internet helps them meet others with comparably liberal sentiments. Tarek is a 30-year-old Jordanian who went to college in London and now works for an American consulting company in Amman. His social circle is full of men and women who feel out of sync with their society. "This is a conservative society, where young people feel sexually deprived," he explained. "Men are always seeking women and women are looking for a discreet relationship." He said the Internet has become a particularly vital tool for single women in his class, who, whether they are 20 or 30 or 40, continue to live with their parents and under a strict curfew. Laila, a 29-year-old banker in Amman, sees the Internet as a possible way around arranged marriages. "Traditionally, mothers, aunts and family friends were the matchmakers," she said. "This tradition has changed somewhat because women now are out in society learning, working, living. Men and women interact, but it still remains that they don't often date. Online dating and interacting with the opposite sex via a computer screen has proven to be a lifeline and a window for many singles here."

Tarek has a rich life full of friends and family who all have their eyes open for the woman who could become his future wife. Sometimes his biggest social struggle is to find time alone. Still, the computer is always on in his office, and he admits he likes the adventure of pursuing unknown women. He has connected with several women this way, usually through the free online chat service ICQ, and he has met a handful of them. According to local online etiquette, people will not usually state their desire for love or romance, instead saying they are looking for friends, and using innuendo to proceed from there. "The search is very simple," explained Tarek. "I search for females living in Amman between the age of 18 and 25. It usually reveals something like 8 or 12 people who are online at that particular moment. You check to see if they want to chat, you chat by instant messenger for a half hour or an hour, and if you develop any mutual interests you decide to go out on a date."

Although the Internet could potentially broaden horizons for people like Tarek, he says the social realities in Jordan make such an approach to Internet dating impractical. "In Jordan, you have the rich minority... and within this minority you have the private school kids where most people have been educated abroad. This society in general is liberal even by Western standards. The rest of the country is very conservative." While it is possible for someone like Tarek to meet more religious women online, he said they usually do not want to take the relationship offline. Recently, he chatted with one woman who told him that she wore a head scarf, a clear sign that she hailed from a more religious background. He did persuade her to meet him at a café, but only after he informed her "beyond any doubt" that he was not seeking a relationship. "These girls are looking for religious guys too. The most important thing they desire in a guy is that he prays," said Tarek. "We went out to a café and just chatted and that was it. She is nice. She is quite cute actually. But you see, she is conservative and so there is no room for any intimate relationship. And she is from a different class so marriage is not possible."

There is one other kind of relationship that is possible for affluent Jordanian men like Tarek to pursue online, but he said it is risky. "There is also a different type of girl here, girls who are in the poorer class of society, whose families might be conservative, but they themselves are liberal. These girls would go out with a guy like me, guys who have a good income, a good status, a car. I can take her out to places, I can help her buy clothes, I can get her a mobile phone and she becomes my partner for two or three months. There is no expectation of marriage unless the girl gets into trouble. You wouldn't marry her, but she could get you into really big trouble or try to blackmail you." Although a man would risk his job this way, Tarek said such relationships are easy to come by online. "In Jordan, a woman is either willing to have a sexual relationship or she is not. If she is not she is not, and if she is, it does not take much effort," he said. "It was different when I was in England, where it was more through a real relationship that men and women would have sex."

Jordan is home to Shafeeq Rushaidat Street in the college town of Irbid, which, according to a recent study by the Rand Corporation, has the highest concentration of cyber cafés in the world. And, as in so many Arab countries, close to half Jordan's population is under the age of 20, suggesting the level of computer proficiency and online interaction is likely to soar. If big American dating services have failed to attract much of this exploding market, the inroads these businesses have made to date have come with virtually no advertising support, no translation into local languages and no attempt to offer any local content. "We've got really high registration in some (Muslim and Arab) countries," said Joe Cohen, who heads Match.com's international business, and says the service is signing up 1,000 new members a day in Egypt and Turkey. Countries like Afghanistan and Iraq are less hip to the international online dating scene, but do produce occasional postings from American military people, foreign aid workers and locals.

When Match.com first took its site international in 1997, it made the decision to offer a start page where visitors could literally search the world over for a mate, and even zero in on such diverse places as Albania, Botswana, Greenland or Afghanistan. But that exhaustive list of choices became something of a joke and many people took it no more seriously than the vast age range Match.com also offered, going all the way up to 120 years. "I think we were being incredibly optimistic," said Cohen, who explained that the company decided to include every last country after a survey revealed that 40 percent of Americans believed there was just one right person for them in the entire world. Internally, however, there were no real expectations of reaching beyond Western Europe or Latin America. In 2001, when the company updated its expansion plans with agreements to launch local sites in 15 countries, there was still not a single Muslim country on the list. "But after seeing the response in countries like Egypt and Turkey, you might be able to make a case for it," said Cohen.

Several things would probably have to change before the company could justify such an investment. Although a fair number of city dwellers in the Middle East can get online in Internet cafés, access remains off limits to the overwhelming majority of the population because of economic, literacy and language barriers. Even in Kuwait, one of the wealthiest countries in the Middle East, only 18.9 percent of the population has access to the Internet. In Egypt and Morocco, penetration is less than 1 percent. Membership fees for U.S. services range from $10 to $25 a month, making them off limits to most people. The average Jordanian, for example, earns about $420 a month, and young singles report that even when they live with their parents, they can barely make ends meet. Those who do have disposable cash often still lack credit cards to arrange for online payment. Talal Abu-Ghazaleh, a Jordanian who heads a task force to help bring the digital revolution to all of the people of the Middle East, says massive work is needed to get the region fully wired. As overall literacy throughout the Arab world hovers at around 50 percent, Internet literacy, which requires computer knowledge and familiarity with English to access any breadth of content, is less than 2 percent, Abu-Ghazaleh estimated. With 80 percent of all Web content in English, there is limited incentive for many people to get connected. "I am a grandfather of seven and a father of four and I don't know a lot about Internet dating," he said. "But if you talk about intelligent use of the Internet for any reason—education, e-commerce, or e-business—there is a big problem with literacy and language."

Censorship is another problem. In 1999 Human Rights Watch completed an exhaustive study of the availability of the Internet in different Arab countries and found that many were blocking large quantities of content. Saudi Arabia, for instance, pledged to block all "undesirable content" when it began offering public access to the Internet in 1999. Ricky Goldstein, who wrote that report three years ago, said more recently that a lot has changed since then. But the change has come mainly because governments in the Middle East, not unlike U.S. Internet service providers trying to combat spam, have lost the battle to block objectionable material originating from ever-changing addresses. While countries such as Egypt and Jordan have been relatively aggressive in building Internet connections, Syria, Libya and Iraq strive to limit Internet access. Bahrain and Tunisia openly monitor Internet traffic. In such places, the rules about what content is allowed are sometimes as blurry as the rules about social interaction between men and women. On the one hand, singles who do socialize online can take comfort knowing that censorship is pretty much a losing battle, with the bulk of objectionable content falling through the cracks. Still, many of these governments are opposed to sexually explicit material on the Internet, as well as politically subversive text, and have from time to time made an example of violators they managed to catch. In 2001, Tunisian authorities arrested the editor of the online publication *Tunexine*, seizing him from the cyber café where he wrote his screeds. "It seems to show the government's determination to keep the Internet from becoming a refuge for free expression," said Hanny Megally, executive director of Human Rights Watch's Middle East division. Young Muslims who are part of the online dating scene say there are some unspoken limits on their behavior, although no one is sure what those limits are. "Is it controversial? Dating per se is controversial," explained one editor at an Arabic language Web site. He added, however, that he had three friends in Saudi Arabia who had met their spouses online.

One of the most intriguing places where Muslim singles converge is a site with the intuitive name MuslimSingles.com. There, photos of heavily made-up women with big hair sit alongside those of women whose faces and necks are tightly cloaked in head scarves.

Suggestive introductory lines like "Smooth As Silk" follow straightforward ones like "To a gentleman serious about marriage." The MuslimSingles site, part of the GeoSingles network of dating sites, which also offers sites for Buddhist Singles, Lutheran Singles, Atheist Singles and Bahai Singles, does not appear to take any stance about the correct way to observe the faith.

Another site, with the similar name of SingleMuslim.com, however, does. Rather than asking members to list their weight or their favorite sport, this site requires that they specify how many times a day they pray, and for female members, whether or not they cover their heads. All who join must also write a line or two describing their relationship with Allah. "I want my relationship with Allah to get better and to get closer to Allah every day until I die," said a 41-year-old Saudi Arabian man, who described himself as a serious Muslim who nonetheless liked to have fun. While bigger American dating sites offer light content about flirting or tips about launching a specialized search, the SingleMuslim.com site features articles such as "Polygamy: Is It Allowed?" This piece proposed that the practice of polygamy, started by the Prophet at a time when there was a large number of widowed women and orphaned children, still had relevance today in places such as England, where there are only 97 males for every 100 females. The site also offers a strong point of view. An article it featured on "The Girlfriend-Boyfriend Relationship," began with this: "In Islam, there is no such thing as a girlfriend-boyfriend relationship. You are either married or you are not." SingleMuslim.com does not require women to observe the Hijab, or wear head coverings, but it endorses the practice. "Imagine being so scared of rejection that you refuse to show your real face in public," reads one editorial on the site. "Imagine being so scared of having your brain and personality discovered that you squash yourself into bras that elevate your breasts and wear underwear that give your butt extra oomph so that attention is painfully drawn away from the heart."

Some of the members of SingleMuslim can imagine. Although the site outlines guidelines for ultra-modest dating, it curiously does not completely ban women from posting their photos with their makeup, or without scarves. A 30-year-old Moroccan woman posted a photo of herself in a red polka dot dress, saying she was a recent convert to Islam and planned to eventually cover up but had not done so yet. SingleMuslim.com is available to Muslims the world over, but the overwhelming majority of its 8,000 plus paying members come from some of the most open societies in the world, such as the United States, Canada and Britain. Just as the Internet has become an outlet for liberated people living in closed societies, it is also a means of control for conservative people living in the West. Many who list themselves on SingleMuslim.com say that connecting over the Internet reassures them they are not becoming physically intimate. "Yes, there is some controversy over Internet dating," said a spokeswoman for the Arab Marriage Connection, which produces the site. "We feel that the Internet is just a place to meet the person. Investigation of the person is still necessary."

If this mix of conservative and secular, covered-up and low-cut, burka and lipstick, seems like a contradiction to an outsider, those within these disparate communities in the Muslim world respond with a shrug. Mona Kanhani, a Jordanian-American who works at the Arabic-language Internet portal Shuf.com in Sunnyvale, California, said it is the diversity of the Internet that makes online matchmaking work so well. "A religious person will find another religious person on the Internet. That is easy," she argued. "We have a lot of normal people posting ads on our site, but we also get those weirdoes who post themselves naked, and we have to delete them." Overall usage patterns on Shuf.com, an Arabic word that means "look," reveal just how many of the Arabs who log on to the Internet do so looking for love or sex. Although Shuf was set up as a general Arabic search engine with a range of discussion categories from business to education, about eight out of ten visitors gravitate to the discussion forum on life and love. Shuf also offers a personals section that has become particularly popular in Syria, where many locals, perhaps less savvy about online dating etiquette, post little else than their names and email addresses, making one ad virtually indistinguishable from the next.

Between the sex-starved and the sex-crazed, the digerati and the barely literate, though, there is a solid base of middle-of-the-road types, like the Iranian women Dorri and Maheen, who are a little bit intrigued by the West, but in the end not entirely comfortable mingling online. After corresponding with different men, Dorri finally zeroed in on an Iranian man living abroad who told her that he missed his country and would like to meet her during a trip home. Too uneasy to tell her parents about her date with this strange man who had identified himself only by the color and license plate number of his rental car, she secretly went to a restaurant to meet him, but did not know how to conduct herself. "We spent some time in the restaurant, and then took a drive to the mountain, but not so far up, because I had a headache," she said, careful to note that she had not so much as touched the man all day. "In our religion we can't have sexual intercourse with a man who is not our husband. Of course, I can't say all Iranian people pay attention to these rules, but I feel very bad if I want to have this kind of relation with a man who is not my husband."

7

WILL IT SELL IN SHANGHAI?

"Why don't you write to me? There is nothing much I can say about myself in this forum but this narrative must contain at least one hundred characters, so I've decided to write that I have nothing to write. So is that enough by now?"

—A 30-year-old Chinese man

Tucked behind Hong Kong's bustling banking district is Lan Kwai Fong, a low-rise strip of Irish pubs, hamburger joints and nightclubs frequented by Westerners in town on business or holiday and looking for familiar food and a little bit of familiar barroom banter. These days, though, it is not at all difficult to encounter people who are visiting town for more intriguing personal business, like meeting their Internet brides.

One warm afternoon in March, a disheveled 61-year-old Irishman named Gerry wandered into a Lan Kwai Fong pub that was offering a pre-St. Patrick's Day buy-one-get-one-free special on Guinness pints. To the thin afternoon crowd consisting of the bartender, a journalist and a couple of expatriate patrons, Gerry described the whirlwind his life had become in the three weeks since he had stepped off the plane. Recently retired, Gerry had dipped into his life savings and traveled halfway around the world to meet a 38-year-old Chinese woman whose acquaintance he had made online just four months earlier. In no time, Gerry had been whisked up to meet the woman's extended family, who all shared a cramped high-rise apartment in a working-class section of the city. He had taken her out to dinner every night since. The relationship appeared to be progressing at an accelerated pace. Three weeks after they first laid eyes on each other, there was serious talk of marriage. Gerry seemed to think it was the right thing, and he said that his new girlfriend definitely agreed. And in their limited English, all the relatives who lived with her in the apartment across the harbor seemed to be giving their tacit approval as well.

There is a simple explanation for this scenario, and Internet dating companies are practiced at rehearsing it. People, they argue, are the same from Belfast to Beijing, all looking for love and willing to travel the world to find it. The online dating business that has exploded in the United States can work just about anywhere. That American online dating sites have managed to gain traction in some of the most conservative Arab countries seems to speak volumes about their opportunities in other, more open, societies. "The world is more similar than it is different," argues Match.com's Joe Cohen. Overseeing an expansion into 25 countries, including France, Korea and New Zealand, Cohen has one of the busiest jobs in the company. Although Match remains leery about entering predominately Muslim countries, it believes that many other cultures are ripe for online dating. "Every culture has a history of third-party intermediaries acting as matchmakers," says Cohen. When Match.com set out to gauge the level of interest in its service around the world to consider where it might prudently invest in local sites, it found little reason to hesitate. Business was getting big not just in some predictable spots like England, but also throughout

Western Europe, Japan and many parts of Asia. In India, and among Indian emigrants worldwide, there were signs that online dating was supplanting some of the small matchmakers who have for centuries provided assistance to families trying to marry off their children. It was growing rapidly in Eastern Europe, too, and in many of the less wired and less wealthy regions of Latin America. "Colombia shocked me the most," said Cohen, who discovered that although just one million of the country's 41 million residents were Internet users, 16 percent of that small wired base had joined its service. This meant close to one in six of the people with Internet access in Colombia were using Match.com, just one of a multitude of dating services available to them.

China is not yet a country of focus for most U.S. dating sites, but they are eyeing it with interest. It would seem foolish not to. China's population of at-home Internet users recently surpassed Japan's to become the world's second largest, ranking behind only the United States. More enticing to the dating companies is all the room for growth still left. When it passed Japan's in 2002, China's wired community represented just 5.5 percent of its total population, so it is only a matter of time before its online community is the world's largest. Already, in major Chinese cities like Hong Kong, Beijing and Shanghai, it is relatively easy to find young Chinese who met their spouses online, and many more who, like their skittish American counterparts, have had a couple of casual online dalliances. Even Chinese from rural parts of the country have used online dating services to find spouses abroad.

America Online's ICQ online community has always been a leading place to form international friendships and for people from countries with limited online resources, such as Belarus, to connect with others locally. Even the name "ICQ" reflects the site's mission as a place to find people, rather than data; it is the phonetic version of the phrase "I seek you." But as the longstanding practice of forming casual online pen pals has evolved into one where aggressively seeking romance is accepted behavior, ICQ has shifted the emphasis of its Web site from a place for friends to one for lovers. Today it features an "ICQ wedding album," spotlighting a multiethnic assortment of couples. With more than 150 million registered users around the world, almost 80 percent of whom are under the age of 30, ICQ is in an ideal position to launch a worldwide dating site. It too recognizes the importance of tapping the massive Chinese population. Today, after years of attracting visitors the world over almost effortlessly, ICQ has stepped up efforts to build up its base of users within select countries, and it recently picked China as the first country to host a local ICQ Web site. ICQ, based in Israel, saw the move into China as a good test of how universal the online dating model really is. "We wanted to choose something very remote and see how it did," said Amit Shafrir, vice president of operations at ICQ. Already, its wedding album features a number of American-Chinese matches, like that of Craig Durbin and NaNa Huan, who say they fell in love over a series of online chat sessions, met after a year of emailing and soon after that, became engaged. Others in the ICQ wedding album hail from Germany, Taiwan, Canada, Turkey, Egypt and Trinidad.

Still, the business of romance does seem to get more complicated the farther one strays from home. Not even the haze of new love could free Gerry, the 61-year-old Irishman, from a little cynicism toward his eager bride. When he wandered into that Hong Kong pub at two o'clock in the afternoon just a week before he was scheduled to return home, he seemed to be seeking the rational advice of some peers. And as chance would have it, one of the few other people there was an English-speaking immigration lawyer, who said he had heard the same story many, many times before. He quickly reminded Gerry of all the reasons other than true love that might lead a woman of limited means to race to the altar with a much older man she had just met. As the beer, and then the shots, flowed, the lawyer questioned Gerry about his limited interaction with his bride to be, asked how much information she had gleaned about his personal finances, how much pressure her family had placed on the idea of marriage. Gerry sighed. A good bit on both counts, it turned out. When Gerry finally wandered back out into the balmy Hong Kong evening, he said nothing about a change of heart, but appeared to be a little bit less set on marriage than he had been just hours earlier.

That such a scenario would unfold in Hong Kong says a lot about how pervasive the desire to marry a stranger from abroad, for money, may be worldwide. By world standards, Hong Kong is a fairly prosperous place. Shiny corporate skyscrapers as well as massive malls offering an extensive selection of designer clothing to rival New York or Paris are plentiful. Not all locals frequent this gold-paved part of the city; most live in more shabby high-rises whose facades are stained by years of pollution. Still, homelessness is all but nonexistent and per capita income is close to $24,000 a year—less than the $35,000 in the United States but almost exactly equal to what it is in Ireland, and well above the per capita income of $860 in mainland China.

But Hong Kong also has one of the highest costs of living in the world and is more densely populated than any other urban area. Many residential high-rises look even from the outside to be squeezed beyond capacity, with rows of laundry and other personal items hanging from the windows, and locals will explain that the reason you see no homeless on the street is that many of the modest two- and three-bedroom apartments towering overhead house several generations of family, who have no other affordable place to live, unless they move abroad. Gerry's Hong Kong girlfriend might have had nothing less pure than true love on her mind, but generally speaking, if Western dating services are having surprising success in some of the world's poorer cultures, the explanation seems to be mercenary as often as it is romantic.

It is not China, though, but Russia, that seems to have produced the most aggressive online community of women seeking to escape shabby living conditions through marriage. To the extent that Western dating services have penetrated the market in Russia and other former Soviet republics, they have attracted the most seriously marriage-minded women, as well as some American men who, having exhausted all the options at home, are often just as desperate. If Russian women have been misled into believing there is an abundance of handsome and wealthy American men who cannot find a wife at home, the men who seek them sometimes have the impression that all Russian women are willing to throw standards out the window. Services that specialize in U.S.-Russian introductions play on both stereotypes, sending out spam mailings bearing messages like this: "Tired of Dating Spoiled American Women? Russian Women are Unspoiled, Devoted and Grateful." Another ad for a Russian mail-order bride service offers this letter from a woman who calls herself Olga: "I live in Russia and I am looking to get out, as I have no future here. I have no good work here, and for me, all the men here drink a lot or do not treat women good." Many also push the idea that Russian women are just more attractive than Americans, noting that poverty helps them keep their waistlines. Because they usually cannot afford cars, these ads explain, many Russian women are forced to walk everywhere.

Businesses connecting Western men with Russian women run the whole gamut from scam artists to legitimate dating services. Those on the more legitimate end of things point out that Russian women are not as desperate as they are often presented to be, and are not willing to settle for the first man who will pay for her trip out. John Adams, who in 1995 founded A Foreign Affair, offering bachelor tours of Russia, argues that his service is nothing more than a way for American men to expand their pool of options and meet some women who often are more grateful, and yes, often thinner, than their American counterparts. Despite a high-profile case in which a Washington state man was convicted of killing his 20-year-old bride from Kyrgyzstan, Adams says there is no evidence suggesting domestic violence is any more common than in traditional marriages between two Americans. Likewise, he has found that although Russian women will not always settle for any man who can get them out of their country, many are, after years of living in an oppressively chauvinistic culture, quite open to taking a chance on a man from abroad. "It is a combination of factors," says Adams, who himself is happily married to a Russian woman he met through one of his tours. "A better economic life, being treated better, and the fact that a lot of Russian men are being treated for alcoholism." Adams's company offers trips to Russia designed so that 20 or 25 single American men can, while staying in nice hotels and eating good food, meet about 200 Russian women. Such groups often advise male clients on how to pursue a correspondence with strange women who do not speak their language, and how to help women obtain "fiancé visas" for extended travel to the United States when a mutual interest seems to be established.

Natasha Kolb, a 26-year-old computer project manager who has lived in Palo Alto, California, since her family emigrated from Russia ten years ago, says that as a fully Americanized adult, she can appreciate the plight that has led many of her girlfriends in Russia to consider becoming mail-order brides. "I think the majority would marry just to leave the country," she said. "In this point in Russia, the man is the head of the household and you have to feed him and do everything for him, and it's not that great. There are not that many women who have jobs, and for those who do, there are not any sexual-harassment laws. Your boss can harass you as many times as he wants, demand that you sleep with him if you want to keep your job." Still, Kolb says that some of her friends who have attended the bachelor tours have, after seeing the selection of men, determined to stay in Russia after all. Although she knows some mail-order brides who fell in love, she says many more of the marriages she has observed seem doomed from the start, either because the bride saw the marriage as nothing more than a ticket out, or, upon coming to America, discovered that she liked the macho ways of Russian society more than she thought.

Although this mail-order bride business has flourished on the Internet, it is really not an Internet dating business at all. It is more an old-fashioned way of connecting people, mainly through tours or catalogs of pictures, not unlike those American matrimonial services that served men and women of the American frontier in the 19th century. Among the modern conveniences that many people in Russia lack is Internet access. Even traditional mail can be unreliable. Bachelors really intent on finding a bride are advised to send duplicate letters, pay extra for a mail-forwarding service, or even fork over a heftier fee to have their letters translated so they can court a woman in her native tongue. But alongside all this, a number of dating scams involving Russian women have found their way to the Internet—so much so that some Western dating services, including Match.com, say they have had to exclude people from Russia and many former Soviet Republics from their U.S. sites, following complaints from customers in the United States who said many of these women seemed more interested in extorting money than in pursuing a relationship. The scams are generally pretty unsophisticated. Typical were men who said they were talked into sending a woman money for a plane ticket, or a visa application, then never heard from her again.

When companies talk about the promise of online dating internationally, they frequently cite India, not just for its large population, but for its strong tradition of matchmaking, coupled with the large numbers of Indians living outside of India who are eager to find Indian spouses. "There is a huge brokering opportunity," says Meredith Hanrahan of TerraLycos, who finds that although Indians today are not so tied to the notion of arranged marriages as earlier generations might have been, they still face family pressure to get married, often to other Indians. The seriousness with which many in the Indian community approach dating as nothing more than a short road on the way to marriage may be demonstrated by the content on some Indian-specific dating sites, such as Shaadi.com, which offers people just two categories under which to search. No friends or flings for visitors to Shaadi; visitors must search for either a bride or a groom.

TerraLycos believes that the overseas online dating market could eventually be twice the size of the U.S. market, but as it plots its expansion internationally, it is finding that people are really not the same everywhere. Unlike the stereotype of the marriage-minded Indians or the money-minded Russians, people in much of Europe, the company has found, are ultra-casual at least when it comes to Internet dating. "It is a whole different concept in northern Europe," says Kai Groundstroem, a product manager for Lycos Europe who oversees a number of local dating sites, such as Love at Lycos, which is focused on the British market. Groundstroem says that these services have been designed with lighthearted fun rather than serious commitment in mind. Love at Lycos offers only a brief questionnaire and avoids all the hard questions. "We don't go into great detail for people. We don't ask them if they have children, or if they want children," he explains.

Although American dating sites speak knowingly about the potential of the Chinese market, some local Chinese dating sites argue they are naïve to think they can just enter the market without a deep appreciation of all the cultural differences. The popular Chinese-language content site Sina.com says that selling online dating to its audience means targeting a population that is for the most part shyer and less willing to express its desires or proactively sell itself than an American audience. "People are not as aggressive in China," says Jack Hong, vice president of information technologies at Sina. "Ethnic Chinese in general have a tendency to be more passive in terms of selling themselves." Hong says this reserve is probably a holdover from an earlier time when young people of marrying age typically expressed their desire for another individual through their parents, usually not daring to approach their intended or even make eye contact before a formal meeting had been arranged. Although young Chinese today have been exposed through film and television to the more forward ways of the West, tradition dies hard. "They have been educated in being conservative and modest," says Hong. This combination of traits would seem to make it hard to make online dating work, at least the way it works in the United States, where people often write hundreds of words of text highlighting all their attributes. And yet, online dating is one of Sina's most popular services. Originally introduced as a way for Chinese abroad to meet other Chinese, the dating service, loosely translated as "Club Love," is now widely used in Hong Kong and mainland China.

It works a little differently on Sina. "In an American personal ad, people describe who they are and who they are looking for," says Hong. "On Sina they stop with who they are. The burden of being very aggressive is not on the individual." The result is page after page of profiles of single people who are hard to distinguish from one another. They have answered all the questions about their basic characteristics, but offered no additional information. Although some people do, the majority of Chinese on Sina's Club Love provide no photos. Because of what Hong says is a reticence in the Chinese character to being too assertive or boastful, Sina sees its role as an online dating service as more involved than just bringing people together. It also must create more opportunities for them to actually connect. So it has enhanced its dating offering with a kind of blind date service it calls "Love Hunter Express" that helps users winnow down the vast pool of choices to a select few. It also offers a lot of offline dinners and other social events in China and in communities with a large Chinese population around the world, such as Silicon Valley in northern California. Often, these events offer something of a guided tour through the daunting world of dating, setting up tables of men and women and providing written instructions on how to converse and mingle. Chinese who sign up to attend one of Sina's offline dating events are guaranteed not just introductions to the opposite sex, but more than a little handholding. They get a list of sample questions to get the dialogue going: What do you do on the weekend? What restaurant do you like the most? along with instructions on how to proceed. "At the end of the evening," it advises, "find the girl who you liked the most during the conversation. Treat her to a drink if you want."

There is one other big difference between American and overseas online dating practices. Unlike in the United States, where customers have become amenable to paying for online dating, most local services overseas are still free. The Lycos dating sites in Europe currently make money through premium services, like an extended photo album or an online "black book" for keeping track of potential dates, although the company says it remains a major question whether European customers will eventually be persuaded to pay for online dating en masse. In China, too, computer-based dating on services like Sina remains free.

Yet Sina is not worried about how it will make money from its popular online dating service. It is based in a land where mobile phones are ubiquitous, and phones that enable text messaging and color photo sharing are the norm. More and more, Chinese youth willing to try online dating prefer to do it from their mobile phones through a system in which they pay a small fee for every message sent. "It certainly has the potential to be our most lucrative business," says Hong. He adds that mobile dating, which is conducted on the run and provides for more instant back-and-forth communication, is promising for another reason; it more closely resembles the kind of computer games that have attracted legions of young Chinese boys and girls.

If youth in many parts of the world may crowd into cyber cafés for a chance to connect with others through email, the far more popular thing in China is online gaming. While Westerners in Hong Kong are chatting over beers and burgers, local teenagers a few blocks away pass their Saturday nights, their Friday mornings and much of the time in between in dingy gaming clubs, where the shades are drawn, packaged noodles are served and everyone chain smokes while focusing on the screens before them with the intensity of air-traffic controllers. Gaming is serious business in China, and as Sina.com sees it, turning online dating into another game is a sure way to hook new generations. "Dating is really a subset of mobile gaming," says Hong. "It is a real-world game."

8

SEX, COMPANIONSHIP AND CAR REPAIRS

"I can handle a circular saw as well as I can handle any of my kitchen appliances. I really want a diversion from all this remodeling. I work out about 3–5 times a week and am in good shape but all this work and no play has gotten me no 'body' to share the nice body with."

—A 41-year-old Ohio woman

Back in her small New England town, Annabel's social life seemed to be progressing. After dismissing several of the men who had contacted her, she had written directly to the one she had noticed from the start, the bicyclist-turned-clown. "You had me sold with your other photo," she said in her email. "This new one is a little unusual." Another man might have taken offense with her blunt approach, but Roger took it in stride. He promised to take down the unflattering photo of himself in clown paint. "I am definitely a package," he wrote, "but I am not sure I am THE package for you. When it comes to fixing things around the house, I pick up the phone, not my toolbox."

In no time, they had a rapport going. Roger said he liked nothing better on a sunny weekend than to take a long bike ride; he usually logged thousands of miles in a summer. Annabel had to confess that a good summer for her was a few hundred miles. She was slowed down by child-care demands, and by some fierce dogs that ran along her bike route; a couple of times, she had resorted to taking along chunks of raw meat to keep the dogs at bay.

At that, she could almost hear Roger's chuckles coming back at her through the computer. He asked if she had ever considered that perhaps the dogs were running after her in the first place because they had smelled the meat. He signed his message "eHugs."

After several more pleasant exchanges, Roger asked for her picture. Annabel, suspicious as ever, sent her home phone number instead. They spoke and learned that they had a lot in common: divorce, three children apiece, jobs in education, a love for the outdoors. They were both busy preparing for the holidays, but seemed to think they could carve out some time to meet for lunch. Then, Roger stopped calling. His change of heart was very abrupt and Annabel could only go back to their last conversation. She had told him that while she technically had shared custody of her children, her ex rarely showed up to relieve her, even during his scheduled visits every other weekend. Roger had gotten off the phone in a hurry.

"I must be too honest and it frightens some," she said, several weeks later, when she had still not heard back about a lunch date. "Just mentioning 'light' facts—the three young kids, the ex not being a parent 50 percent of the time—it may send some running. He was probably imagining a harried-looking housewife with no time for anything ever. Kind of true, although I don't look like a harried housewife." Annabel sighed. "You know, I still look good. I just bought myself a pair of jeans at the same store where I shop for my 10-year-old daughter. Dammit, I still look good."

Annabel was disappointed, but there was no time to stew. In her already airtight schedule, another crisis had arisen. Annabel's car, a car that was not all that old, had broken down and when she took it to the shop to be repaired, the mechanic told her it could not be fixed. Seemed she had neglected to get regular oil changes and the engine had died. Just 80,000 miles on the odometer, but the car was gone. "Two things I'm learning about myself," she said. "I wish I had a brother, and I like to be cared for when it comes to home improvements. Hell, life in general too."

It was a while before Annabel had time to tend to her email, and when she did, all she could think to do was vent her frustration. She called up her own profile, and on the place where she had specified her preference for sex, companionship and a handyman, she added, "and someone who can help me buy a new car."

Not that she had honestly expected any of these strange men to take her seriously, to show up at her door and instruct her on the sly ways of used-car salesmen. But once again, Annabel's inbox filled up with letters from literal-minded men who either volunteered to accompany her on a trip to the car dealership or just offered some no-strings-attached advice. "In order to buy a car," one wrote, "you must first find out how much it costs the car dealer. My suggestion is to buy a consumer guide book and then write away for the dealer's invoice price. It costs $11 and can save you thousands. You don't need a man to do this, but if you have trouble, I'll lead you. Good luck, you can do it!"

James Hong's holidays were not so frenetic. Life in general remained pretty low key for the not-yet-30-year-old bachelor with the new Porsche and the low-maintenance business. HotOrNot was practically running itself, and the success stories were flowing in. Every time Hong and his partner Jim Young checked their email, there were more fan letters from HotOrNot subscribers, some of them not yet 20, who had found love on the site.

Dear Jim and James, I don't really know how to thank you guys for having this site because if it weren't for the two of you I would have never met the man I have for so long dreamed about. You guys have definitely changed my life.

Hey there J&J, I just have to say that my life couldn't be better right now thanks to you guys. I met the love of my life. We've been dating since August and on Nov. 3rd we decided to be a couple. I am the happiest guy ever right now because I have a great girlfriend. Thanks to you guys!

I just wanted to write you guys and tell you thank you. If it wasn't for HorOrNot, me and my girlfriend Sara would have never met. I have never felt this way towards a girl before, and I am the happiest I have been in my life. We've only been dating about 2 months but it feels like we have known each other our entire lives. We even went ring shopping last weekend!

James Hong could not have been more delighted that his little business was bringing so much happiness into people's lives. It just seemed strange. All around him people were logging on for love, making it all seem so effortless, and he had yet to find a single date through the Internet. Figuring he was too old for the HorOrNot scene that was populated mostly by teenagers and people in their very early twenties, Hong had joined one of the larger dating services. Yet, after several months, he had not heard from anyone, and none of the 15 or so women he had written to had written him back. While everyone else seemed to be finding a girlfriend or a boyfriend, or getting hitched for the holidays, he had received the equivalent of a lump of coal in his online dating stocking: a bunch of spam mail from porn sites.

Julie Fitzpatrick did not find a date for Christmas either. Instead, she found more men who, despite having joined a psychologically focused dating service, behaved like emotional cripples. Most of the men she encountered on eHarmony had breezed through what was supposed to be a thoughtful application, responding that they had never thought about who the most influential person in their life was, that they had no idea what their most striking characteristic was, had not a clue about the best way to make them smile. "I thought it was ridiculous," she said. "I mean, even if I had to think about it, I would think about it, while I was filling out the application." She opted to terminate communication with all of the men that eHarmony had sent her way, except for a single one, who had filled out all the questions with some thought. He sounded intelligent and kind, career and family-oriented. She called up his photos, including one shot underwater while he was scuba diving. "Bushy-haired with a balding hair line," she shrugged. She was in no rush to meet him. As soon as she had gone online to find dates, her offline social life had mysteriously started to pick up. One friend had found a blind date for her, and she had by chance run into an old crush who had invited her away for the weekend. With new possibilities swirling, eHarmony was becoming less of a priority. "I guess I just don't like forced situations," she said.

On Martha's Vineyard, Angelo DiMeglio was not even seeing any possibilities. There were never any new faces in town during the long winter. He had declined some invitations and spent New Year's Eve at home alone, watching a fireworks display from his back deck. The passage of another uneventful year had put him in a melancholy mood, and as he surveyed the stark winter scenery, he began to reflect that his entire life sometimes felt like one long 45-year dry spell. There had been some girlfriends, but they were all in the distant past. Even his last fling was now a distant memory. Youth had turned to middle age, and DiMeglio found himself in that position of waking up one day and not quite knowing how it had turned out this way, a life of such isolation. He thought a lot about his youth as a "long-haired hippie kid" from outside New York City, driving a 1964 Volvo and heading back every chance he could get to the New England island he had fallen in love with. When he first decided to settle there, everything had fallen into

Six months after joining an online dating service, Angelo DiMeglio was still waiting for a date. Reuters.

place: an apprenticeship with a builder who had taught him his trade in a business never short of work, an affordable plot of land where he had built a large house. He had a large extended family and many friends. But over 25 years he had tried everything from blind dates to dating services to dating the college girls who came in the summer, and he could not find anyone who wanted a part of the remote, quiet life he led.

"I built my house 14 years ago hoping to have a wife and children," he said. "I'm not looking for Victoria's Secret, like I used to be. Just a fairly attractive woman who is similar to me who will laugh and be happy. This is a screwed-up place for single people."

He knew that he could not blame the failure of the online dating services for his lack of a social life. But they were certainly no solution to his limited options offline. "I've emailed a few more chicks, and still no response," he said. He had even tried writing to one girl from Sweden who had sounded desperate. She had indicated a willingness to meet someone between the age of 25 and 60. No response. He had contacted another one from nearby Providence, Rhode Island. Nothing. "I don't have much luck with girls," he grumbled. Then he remembered that he had received one response from a woman who told him that he was too old. "I set her up to talk to my brother in New York, but she didn't like him either, because he smokes."

There had not been such a cold snowy winter in years, perhaps decades. Subzero winds swept up and down the eastern part of the country, blanketing Annabel's neighborhood in waist-high snow, and, a little farther to the south, leaving a glaze of ice on Florence's driveway. One morning shortly after the holidays, Florence set out on her daily errands and started to scrape the ice off her car. She slipped and fell flat on her face. At first, she dismissed the injuries as bruises, but later her son insisted she go to the emergency room, where doctors told her she had suffered a broken nose and a sprained knee that she would have to stay off for weeks. In the backyard, her dog ran around restlessly. He missed his regular walks.

While Florence struggled with her physical ailments, her persistence with the online dating was beginning to pay off. After passing over several men whose profiles she thought read like thinly veiled invitations for sex, she had come upon Preston, a 72-year-old man who lived in the next town, and sounded as youthful and family-oriented, and as much of a lover of dogs, as she was. Like all the other men she had come across, he was a nonsmoker. Unlike so many of the others, he said he didn't mind smokers. Florence knew that she might wait forever to hear from this happy-sounding man who still worked full time at the company he had built, so she sent a note off to him, and this time she got a prompt and pleasant response. It might have gone on like that, back and forth over email indefinitely, but Florence still was not very comfortable with computers, and she told him so. She sent him a note suggesting they meet for lunch, adding, "I promise not to smoke in the restaurant." Preston wrote back quickly and said that lunch sounded like a splendid idea.

Finally, in late January, Annabel's ex-husband made good on one of his scheduled weekend visitations, and she found some time to look for the new car she desperately needed. She also caught up on a couple good nights of sleep and a couple of good books. A novel called *The Handyman* had caught her eye, and it seemed to confirm her own need for a big, strong, capable man around the house. "It's a universal theme," she said. "There's something appealing about a man who can fix things. It ranks right up there with the other important stuff." Still, she continued to think about Roger, the anti-handyman, who had seemed like such a nice guy. The rest and relaxation helped Annabel reconsider what had happened. Maybe he had not dismissed her after all. Maybe he was simply a busy dad who had been in a hurry to get off the phone. She decided it would not hurt to send him another email and ask.

"Dear Roger," she wrote. "How were your holidays? Mine were great, but long. I got in some sledding though. I wondered if the small amount of information I shared with you made you run away. Single woman. Three young kids. Yikes. I may feel like a harried housewife at times, but I do not look like one. And I make time for things that are important to me. So you can call or email, Annabel."

9

I'M DYSFUNCTIONAL, YOU'RE DYSFUNCTIONAL

"Is there anyone NORMAL out there?"

—A 23-year-old Florida man

Dara is a pretty 57-year-old artist from Seattle who has an earnest smile and an outdoorsy glow. She was widowed years ago and more recently broke up with her boyfriend of six years. She joined an online dating service and spent a good amount of time writing a detailed and nuanced profile saying she liked old silverware, old houses, old jazz, and wanted a committed relationship. Here are three of the men she heard from:

- One who responded with a one liner: "I love it when you talk dirty."

- A never-married pharmaceutical salesman who sounded interesting enough to meet. They went to a Japanese restaurant where she ordered sushi and he proceeded to inform her about the high mercury content in fish. "Then he pulled a packet of fish oil out of his pocket, opened it up and sucked it down," Dara recalled. "It was kind of disgusting."

- A magazine writer whom she liked well enough to date several times. The relationship seemed to be going well until something happened that made her wonder if she could trust him. One night after they had had dinner together, Dara went home and checked her email and saw that she had received new messages from other men in her dating service. Out of curiosity, she went to the Web site to read about them, but because she was still thinking, fondly, of the man she had been out with that evening, she called up his profile. She saw that he was online too, surfing around the same dating site. She took great offense that he would be so uncouth as to return from a date with her and sit right down at the computer to look for other women.

But Dara herself had been looking at other men, had she not? "Not really," she insists. "I had just happened to check my email and then click through to some of the people who had written to me." Although her date's action may have been equally innocent, she said it left her with a queasy feeling. "We were getting closer and closer to a sexual relationship and I was not about to do that with someone who was going to go back home and log on to a dating site." That night she decided to cool it with the online dating, after concluding that even with the extensive pool of candidates the Internet provided, you could still get stuck with a lot of sex maniacs, cheats and people who drank fish oil for dinner. "I think you'd have to be luckier than the odds on the lottery to win at this game," she said one evening, after several months of active but unsuccessful Internet dating.

Henry, the 40-year-old marketing executive from Denver, does not completely disagree. He has used numerous online dating sites on an off for five years but, many flings and evenings of good conversation later, has yet to find the serious relationship he craves.

(He quit online dating for a year and a half while seeing a girlfriend he met offline, through friends.) Today, Henry continues to go on Internet dates, but he is skeptical. An intelligent and engaging man, he has no problem indulging mystery women in long email conversations, and he says that with the computer as a buffer, he can control his image and be so charming that he often feels the women falling for him before they have met. But he has found that 100 pages of sweet email nothings do not add up to three minutes of face to face. According to one newspaper advice column, some online Romeos are doing more than just crafting perfect prose. "I persuaded a shy male friend to try Internet dating," the advice seeker wrote. "He posted his profile and photo but never actually wrote to anyone. So I got him to let me take over. Now I am courting three women via email in the guise of a 35-year-old man. I am a woman (but, it turns out, I have a way with the ladies). This now feels a bit less innocent, but if it gets my shy friend together with a nice woman, is it wrong?"

Martin, the 38-year-old entrepreneur from New York City who doesn't like paying to subscribe to an online dating service, still likes the wealth of women it provides. Yet he too sees a downside. "It actually is a little bit harmful to society. The Internet just gives you a wonderful reason to move on, like her nose turns too red when she sneezes. People online date to find fault."

At a time when online dating is more popular than ever, it is simply too early to know if it will last. Can the Internet be expected to revolutionize dating as much as the telephone and the automobile did, or as little as those fly-by-night computer dating services that appeared briefly in the late 1960s? For all the success stories in circulation, is success really happening in substantial numbers, relative to all the millions of people who are trying this? It will be a long time before that kind of data appears. Yet anecdotally, some arguments against Internet dating are beginning to pile up for those who care to look deeper than the vast quantity of potential dates it provides.

Joel Ginsberg is a 40-year-old management consultant in San Francisco who was drawn to the Internet because he found the city's offline gay scene a little bit cold and more than a little bit superficial. "All about how you look and how young you are," he said. He had often heard the argument about the Internet being so good for high-achieving professionals like himself who didn't have a lot of time. Once online, however, he discovered that although he didn't need a 20-year-old with a perfectly cut body, he was somewhat into looks himself, and not happy about the Internet as a medium for showing a person's outer beauty. "People don't use very good quality pictures. I mean, I posted photos where you can see my build, a couple of close-ups and a couple of smiley faces. A lot of people give you something where they are 15 percent of the entire field and you can't see anything."

Ginsberg also found all the promises of the Internet as a time-saving tool for busy people to be untrue. "I just find it extremely time consuming," he argued. "It takes a long time emailing to sort of get a sense of who might be interesting if you are looking through ads. You go back and forth several times before you even decide to have a phone conversation. Then finally you plan a time to meet, and after all that, you know within five seconds if there's any potential. If there is not any potential, it's been a waste of weeks of email."

Of course, lying about one's physical appearance is one of the easiest tricks of the Internet, so much so that jokes have been written around the often gaping discrepancy between what someone says and what they mean. Women who say they are 40-ish, the joke goes, are actually 48; if they say they are average looking they are ugly; if they say they are beautiful they are pathological liars. Men who say they are 40-ish, on the other hand, are "52 and looking for a 25-year-old," while those who say they are average looking have "unusual hair growth on ears and nose." In all seriousness, almost anyone who has spent any amount of time Internet dating has a story of the truth not living up to reality, and apparently vanity knows no age limit. Noah, the 84-year-old from Florida, found that "a few extra pounds" as a term to define body type was "grossly abused" among women in their seventies. (Lest people assume that everyone who posts a photo online picks the skinniest one they can find, this headline recently appeared on one dating site, above the full face of a 26-year-old man: "I've lost 100 pounds since this picture was taken.")

Sometimes the exaggerated physical attributes are harmless enough. Ravi, a 38-year-old attorney in Los Angeles, said that when he first met his wife, she was heavier than he had expected. But then, she told him that she had expected he would have more hair. Today they have two children and laugh about their first impressions.

Henry, throughout his five years of Internet dating, says he has come across brutal honesty as much as he has encountered serious deceit. One man who contacted him confessed right away that he was a pre-surgery transsexual. "I wrote back and said I was sure that it was hard for him to tell people, and that I was glad he told me, but it was just not my bag." Another woman sent Henry a pretty photo that did not look at all like the person he arranged to meet in a bar. "I had to say something like, 'Oh, it's so dark in here. I didn't even recognize you.'"

Bernardo Carducci, a professor of psychology at Indiana University Southeast, does not think the lies are always a laughing matter. Carducci, who is director of the University's Shyness Research Institute and offers workshops to help people overcome their social anxieties, said that the Internet seems to prevent people from moving from superficial conversation to deep honesty, the way they almost inevitably do in the offline world. "Here is the problem with the Internet that I found," said Carducci. "When we asked people how true they were in describing themselves, there was really no relationship between the amount of time they had spent interacting and how honest they were. You might think the more time you spend talking to someone online, the more you could trust them, but we found no relation. Offline, there is a check on that."

Common and predictable as these stories of age, height or weight distortion are, many people say, the most troubling things they have encountered online is a kind of emotional distortion: the way Internet dating has, for better or worse, upset their notion of things like flirting and sexual tension. Damon is a 35-year-old graphic artist in Minneapolis, who, after years of trial and error, had built flirting into a science. "I tended to gravitate to the places where I was forced to have an elevator pitch ready," he said, explaining his preference for picking up women in the grocery store, in front of their cars while they were fumbling for change to feed the meter or at a bus stop. "The thrill of being able to impress them not only in a short space of time but in an unknown space of time, to have to present myself as cute and funny and safe in 30 seconds, was a fun challenge. I'd come up with some way to present sexual undertones, but not overtones, lay out a challenge, then wait." Like any guy, he struck out a lot of the time but sometimes he got a date. Then he went online. The first woman he met slept with him. So did the second. The third, he said, wanted to, but he was not attracted to her. It went on like that until at some point, he thought about trawling for men. Although he always presented himself to the world as a straight guy, he'd had a bisexual phase years ago during college and he decided to explore it again. Again more easy success. At first he felt like he had won the lottery: unlimited gay and straight sex, almost on demand. Then he started to feel uneasy. "Now that I know it's easy sex, it's kind of a turnoff," he said. "I don't really go out with these women, I think how fast I can slay them. Now I do less online dating. It takes the fun out of it and it kills your drive."

If people like Damon are turned off by the lack of challenge, others looking for something more lasting find success much more elusive. Some profess a frustration more profound than that which comes from the bar scene, the church group or the extended circle of friends. As the numbers go up, so too does the number of people you would never want to date, or, who would never want to date you. The deep disillusionment you typically suffer over that occasional bad date is multiplied many times over. You need a thick skin to get through it. Martin, the New York entrepreneur on a budget, says that aside from disliking having to pay for all those dates, just the act of going on so many has forced him to become a cynic. It is not that he is opposed to all the volume. His business school degree taught him to see all life's challenges, including affairs of the heart, in terms of risk and reward, investment and return. "As I look at it, if I just went about my normal life I would only have 10 dates a year. With the Internet, I can easily have 100. Over the course of a decade, that's a thousand people I will meet versus only 100 without the Internet," he explains. The problem is that those improved odds come at a price. "You have to go into all of these dates with the feeling of 'No, this is not going to work out.' If you go in with a No, you protect yourself. It's the only way you can do it."

Moreover, because there are so many people to choose from, chances are that not all of them will be as thoughtful as Dara, who crafted serious, individualized letters to everyone she communicated with. Equally common as her approach is the "shotgun" method of sending out multiple one-liner emails saying something generic like "You sound interesting," or something inappropriate like, "I love it when you talk dirty." Strange as it sounds that anyone would try to jump-start a loving relationship that way, many people, and men in particular, confess that the online format reduces them to just that. The odds of any particular woman writing back, they figure, are so slim that they see little reason to invest any time or thought. Overall, the ratio of men to women on online dating sites remains around 60/40, making for a lopsided system in which women's inboxes get stuffed and many great men, like HotOrNot's James Hong, are ignored.

Vernon and Susanna Church found each other online but say they encountered a lot of weirdos first. Reuters.

One person who you'd think could be the poster boy for Internet dating is Vernon Church, a 41-year-old New York City scientist-turned-writer who met his wife, Susanna, through Yahoo Personals four years ago. Susanna came upon Vernon after suffering through just two other bad Internet dates, including one who reminded her of the Unabomber. If three was a charm for her, though, the lucky number for Vernon was much higher. He went out with 99 different women—along the way collecting enough material to write and produce *Connections*, an off-Broadway play about Internet dating—before finally getting lucky with number 100. The happy ending did not erase the memory of all the bad experiences that preceded it. As a result, Vernon Church is not a huge fan of Internet dating.

"By the time I met Susanna, I decided it was a horrible way to meet people," Church said. "It is a really false social environment." Church's first 99 Internet dates led him to conclude that most people who date online either lied about their physical attributes, had a false sense of intimacy and revealed too much too soon, or just had poor social skills that prevented them from meeting people offline. When he met Susanna, he said, it was not love at first sight. But it was noticeably different from all the others.

"It wasn't horrendously bad," he said.

What was so bad about the first 99? "Well, one said, 'I'm not thin like a model but I work out all the time and I'm always in the gym.' When she showed up she probably had 60 pounds on me. She wasn't particularly fat, just big in a linebacker kind of way. She was so sweet but I felt no attraction. It was kind of an awkward situation."

"Then there was a woman who spent the entire date talking about how she had doubled her salary every year for the past five years. If you are even marginally good at arithmetic, you know she was making tons and tons of money. She was talking about how she was going to buy a $5,000 lamp from a feng shui consultant. And then the check came, and she did not even blink." Church picked up the check.

Some of the popular jokes about Internet dating have also addressed this discrepancy between stated personality traits and actual personality flaws. Women who say they are "emotionally secure," one joke goes, are in fact medicated; those who say they are "passionate" are loud; "poet" is code for depressive schizophrenic and "fun" means annoying. Men who say they are "athletic" really mean that they like to sit on the couch and watch ESPN, and those who say they are thoughtful mean that they "say please when demanding a beer." Somewhere between the first Internet date and the one hundredth, Church reached the same conclusion as Judy Storandt in Oklahoma City. Forget the candlelit dinner dates, and meet for a quick coffee in a bookstore café.

"You can say that the reason people are now on the Internet in droves is that no one has the time to meet people offline. However, I really believe that most people are there because they have some social deficit," says Vernon Church. "The reality is that if you are a reasonably secure human being with some social skills, you meet

people." And Church himself? While conceding that he is a "difficult writer type," who is not free of his own social deficits, he says
the main reason he tried the Internet was that he held a managerial
position at work and was therefore not available to date his subor-
dinates. Whatever the reason people first decide to take the online
dating route, he believes that even the most normal, socially
adjusted people can be lulled into an unappealing state of inertia.
"Without the Internet, if you were pining to meet someone you
would, hopefully, get off the couch and go to a party. But the Internet is a totally nonchallenging way to be social."

Delis Alejandro might agree. As a pastoral associate at St.
Monica's Catholic Church in Santa Monica, California, she has
seen more couples than she can count meet and get married
through church functions. Proof, she believes, that even in today's
fast-paced world, there are endless opportunities to meet new faces
if you only circulate. Alejandro oversees multiple parish groups
from a ministry for divorced people to one for gays, another for
lapsed Catholics returning to the church, and several programs to
reach out to the poor and imprisoned. She says there is a social
component to all these activities. "Even if you sign up to help feed
the poor, you are partly doing it to meet people."

Nor is everyone so disillusioned with what has come to be
widely disparaged as "the bar scene." People who look for dates
online commonly say they are tired of the bar scene, which seems to
suggest a place full of sleazy people in search of sleazy sex. This
could be one of the biggest myths to grow out of the online dating
explosion, that attempting to socialize in a bar is foolhardy or passé
and that there are no sincere people who also enjoy unwinding in
public watering holes. Shoshana Lombardi, a 32-year-old who
works in public relations in Washington, D.C., met her husband in
a bar several years ago and remains a big advocate of a venue where
people can casually mingle with others from their community while
dulling their social anxieties with drink. Lombardi's own story of

meeting her husband, Chris, is one of coincidence and mysterious intervention by a third party. She was in the bar in the first place only because she and her friend had gone to the wrong address, missing the bigger party they had meant to attend. As it turned out, one of Shoshana's colleagues was one of Chris' roommates and she seemed intent on getting them together. "She said to me, 'I heard you met my roommate, Chris. He told me that he wanted to see you again,'" Shoshana remembers. "Then she told him that I had said I wanted to see him again, even though I hadn't."

They never did learn the motives behind the woman who was not particularly close to either one of them, but the nudging worked. Still, Lombardi says it was definitely "the bar scene" that gave birth to the initial attraction. She had noticed her future husband from across the bar, thinking nothing so serious as "that is the man I will marry some day." What she thought in her Friday night kick-back mode was, "that is a man who looks a lot like Ferris Bueller," or more precisely, Matthew Broderick, who had played him in the 1986 film *Ferris Bueller's Day Off*. Because she was in a bar and had drunk a couple of cocktails, she giddily called across the bar, "Ferris Bueller! Ferris Bueller!" Finally, he came over to ask why she was screaming at him.

"I have to tell you," says Lombardi, who is only an occasional drinker, "I am a huge proponent of meeting people in bars. Some people think it might not be a place to meet genuine people. But I wouldn't have met my husband if I hadn't been in a bar. And I probably would never have talked to him if I hadn't been drinking."

Such stories of meetings in traditional offline dating venues do prompt the question of whether Internet dating is actually a solution to the impersonal society so many people claim we have become, or just one more isolating factor for a country where individuals are already sequestering themselves in home gyms, home offices or in airtight automobiles while driving solo to the office. Professor Carducci says his own research has located a clear link between technology and social avoidance. "The Internet has not only given us more access and information, it has created a sense of hyperculture," he said. "The speed at which our culture operates is getting faster and faster. As things get faster, people lose patience. In order to be noticed, you have to be more extreme and louder, and that works against a lot of people who get pushed out of the way." Carducci does not see the Internet or Internet dating as the whole problem. He notes that people in their twenties and younger grew up with the Internet and use it, like the telephone, as a logical extension of their social development. And he says many other factors, like the growth in gated communities, are contributing as much as the Internet to the sense of isolation. Trend watcher Faith Popcorn recently came up with the term "cocooning" to describe a social phenomenon in which four million Americans were living in gated communities, 16.6 million had their own private movie theater and more than 10 million were telecommuting. But within these realities, the Internet provides one more way to avoid face time. "When you have thousands of people doing it, there is some probability of success," argues Carducci. "Of course, if you were to approach thousands of people on the street, you could probably find someone to go out with you too."

Which gets back to that story of Vernon Church and his 100 online dates. Might he have found a wife anyway if he had taken such a systematic approach offline? "A wife or two, I'd say," he responded quickly. "Seriously, I suspect it would have taken much less time in real space. Neither person would bother to pursue someone in that context whom they didn't find attractive in the first place. More importantly, in the real world you find the usual amount of neurosis. In contrast, the anonymity of the online environment selects for people who have difficulties with meeting people face to face. That dysfunction can take many forms—inability to communicate, fear of intimacy, narcissistically high standards. On the street, on a good day, you would simply pass those people by, socially speaking. That's not to say that everyone online is socially challenged, just that one finds a larger percentage of people who are."

His explanation might help explain some of the random and odd responses that Sally, a 37-year-old graduate student in Los Angeles, received when her friends persuaded her to try online dating. One frightened her right off the bat when he wrote to say that he had wonderful relationships that were based on "good conflict resolution." Another said, in his introductory letter, that he was very good friends with his ex and had "other friends as well." Yet another sent a nude photo along with separate close-ups of particular body parts. Finally, a fourth suitor sounded nice enough in print, and she gave him her phone number. He called and asked within the first five minutes what she looked like in a bathing suit. A second man who got her phone number made repeated, pleading phone calls over the course of several months, leaving messages like, "I'm tall and fit, and better looking than my photo."

Like Professor Carducci, many psychologists who specialize in social anxiety say they encourage shy and apprehensive patients to use the Internet as a way to meet new people in a relatively non-threatening environment. They also warn that technology can exacerbate existing problems, enabling very shy people to avoid confronting their fears while giving others license to be rude and inappropriate from behind a screen of anonymity. "Shy people often go to the Internet," said Jonathan Berent, a psychologist based in Great Neck, New York, and the author of *Beyond Shyness*. "The increase in technology is making social avoidance easier than ever before. People have always been able to avoid other people by sitting in a room and watching television or calling phone sex lines, but the Internet raises the bar, creating the impression that they are interacting, but not requiring that they do any of the hard work in terms of dealing with people face to face."

Merri, the New York City journalist who found her husband on her second Internet date, sees it differently. She too had one bad Internet date. "He was a total loser, weirdo, creepy guy," she says. "I was so demoralized and depressed, but I decided to keep doing it." And that perseverance ultimately led her to adopt a more positive take on the online dating jungle. As she sees it, one of the best things about Internet dating is that it lets you move on from your disappointments more quickly. "Everyone knows you have to kiss a lot of frogs to meet your prince, but the Internet speeds up that process," she said. "You can go through nine frogs in two weeks rather than two years."

When Match.com successfully paired up Alex Siegel, a San Jose, California, engineer, and his wife Rochelle, a teacher's assistant, it got more than it bargained for: five success stories. After the Siegels married in 1998, Rochelle gave birth to triplet boys, Ethan, Avery and Justin. Could there possibly be a more wholesome online dating success story? Match.com seems to think not. As part of its promotional material, the company distributes an adorable photo of the three toddlers sitting upright in three boat-like plastic laundry baskets, navigating their living room floor. Curiously, though, neither Rochelle nor Alex is the most enthusiastic supporter of online dating. Rochelle, who joined Match.com in 1997, when she was still in college at a California State University and the Internet was a much smaller place, says she probably would not do it again today, because she thinks the Internet has become more frightening as its ranks have grown.

Like his wife, Alex also has measured enthusiasm for online dating. On the plus side, he notes, it is a lot better than the offline dating services he used back in upstate New York when he was a graduate student at Cornell University. "They had this sort of big room full of binders that had the applications of women you would go through to look for one that seemed suitable, and then you would call her," he explained of the offline service Great Expectations. "It was pretty awkward." Alex Siegel had multiple dating service horror stories, including one that was not the fault of the dating service at all, in which he lost part of his leg in a motorcycle accident and seriously injured the woman he had just met earlier that evening. "We never talked again," he said.

Aside from that tragedy, Siegel said, there was no denying that the people who joined dating services, at least in upstate New York, were a motley crew. "There are a lot of people who use dating services because they have to," he said. "I guess either they are very awkward, or they are very weird, or they have some particular hang-up, or something incredibly specific they are looking for." Then, including himself in the group he just described, he added, "I was a computer geek, so I wasn't very good at meeting people." Siegel said that when he began using online services, the pool of people was much larger, the quality better and the system of emailing before you called or met made him a lot more comfortable. "The Internet is better than a normal dating service," he said, before adding one admonition. "You do have to be very careful because there are a lot of fairly dangerous creeps online."

Spoken like an expert. But what did he, a conservative engineer and father of three, know about the creepy men online?

"What they typically do is tell women they are young and handsome and rich, and when they actually meet them, they are not."

And how did he know that?

"Well," Siegel explained. "I've spent a lot of time in chat rooms. And for a little while my brother and I had this game we would play. We would get online and pretend to be 22-year-old beautiful college girls just out looking for a good time and we would see how many guys we could get going at the same time and try to tease them along. It was tremendously easy to get tremendous numbers of people interested in you."

Because Dara, the artist from Seattle, was not a person to give up easily, she finally erased the memory of the fish-oil drinker and the guy who wanted to talk dirty, and went back online. It got better. She widened her search and came upon a man from Portland, Oregon, with whom she shared numerous things from single parenthood to a passion for the arts, and a love of the written word. Their emails back and forth were long and thoughtful, at once intellectual and erotic, and you could just tell that they would hit it off. Theirs was a highbrow correspondence. Just in the process of describing her day-to-day life, Dara quoted a line from one of Shakespeare's more obscure plays. She confessed that while she was passionate about her work, she had never achieved great success, since she was more passionate about her children. He responded with a long confessional of his own, describing the moment of his daughter's birth when his "body was drained of conflict and, like a dam bursting, a flood of emotions, joy relief and love, washed over me." She wrote back to compliment him on the difficult choices he made to sacrifice a promotion at work to spend more time with his two daughters.

Each letter was hundreds and hundreds of words of intelligent prose packed with references to literature, family and loneliness. It was becoming so intimate that Dara was starting to like this man, in ways other than just as a potential date. She even suggested that he might like to meet her son, who lived just outside of Portland. She was getting the feeling that she had found a solid friend, if not a lover. They were really connecting, and after several more revealing letters Dara felt it safe to share the stories of some of her less positive online dating experiences. He wrote back to say that he was sorry she had had some bad experiences, his had all been positive, without exception. She wrote in response that there was no need to apologize, she had just been making conversation. In the midst of a very warm letter that had mentioned holiday plans and sent good wishes for the New Year, she happened to add that she was curious to see whether he was writing to her out of sincere interest, or because he had been unable to meet any women in Portland. If nothing else, they were email buddies at this point and it seemed like a fair question. He did not think so. The final letter Dara received from him was the shortest of any of them, and it was the last. "There's a caustic tone in recent exchanges that I find unsettling," he said, "so I think I'm interested no longer."

10

INFIDELITY, INC.

"I'm another guy trying to find that one lady who is seeking to have a good time with a safe, clean, married guy. No strings, just some hot lovin' on your time, not mine. During the day is best for me, however."

—A California man

The NSHM crowd tends to come out after dark. After the family has gone to sleep, they settle down at the computer and search for others like themselves. Some are experienced at the game and automatically post ads describing their angst and their desire for a temporary escape. The boldest among them even post photos. Others move more tentatively, not knowing how they have found themselves here, on an Internet dating site, when they haven't been single in 5, 10 or perhaps 20 years. They swear they want nothing more than a sympathetic ear, someone they can trust not to betray a confidence. Yet even the most apprehensive are quickly made to feel at ease once they discover the extensive community of others just like them who show no guilt or discomfort. In messages typed back and forth and sent into the night, they tell of marriages gone stale, husbands who feel more like brothers, strained commitments to stay together because of the children. For some, the short-term solution to their marital sadness is cyber sex with a stranger from another country. Others look closer to home for someone they might meet, another person just like them who is NSHM, or "not-so-happily married."

Of course, married people found ways to cheat long before they were able to communicate over the Internet. And the easy access to affairs that the Internet provided through email and chat rooms, pretty much from day one, has by now been so thoroughly exposed it hardly warrants any further discussion. But the rise in Internet dating as a real and quite profitable industry has created something new for the unfaithful: a legitimate forum where they can pay to find others who are interested in having an extramarital affair. In a lower-tech time, the unhappily married men or women might have had to wait for an out-of-town business trip until they could act on their desire, or be forced to try something much more awkward and risky, like holding the glance of the person they desired in front of all the neighbors at the local coffee shop. Things like newspaper personals and Internet chat rooms expanded their options almost infinitely, but there was still something hush-hush about having an affair. More recently, a number of online dating businesses have lowered the bar further, essentially by selling memberships to clubs for the not-so-happily married. Large numbers of people are signing up, admitting that they are unfaithful or wish to be. As a consumer group they are a major source of income for some of the largest Internet dating sites. As a demographic group, they seem to be influencing a change in some long-held attitudes in the United States about monogamy and infidelity. During the 1970s it became acceptable for the Single White Female or the Single Black Male to post an ad for love. Today, there are so many people who are not single at all, but just as hungry for love, that they have an acronym too.

The NSHM label actually belongs to the British online dating site uDate.com, which was recently acquired by Interactive Inc., the same company that owns Match.com. While Match.com works hard to keep all its content rated G and kicks off any people who admit to being married, uDate offers something very different. On the uDate registration, under marital status, there are several options, from single to married and all the gray areas in between: engaged, divorced, separated, "married but we swing" and "not so happily married." These categories have attracted members like Evan, a 36-year-old who posted his photo and explained that the spark had left his marriage after his third child was born. Diane, a 44-year-old married for 19 years, is also a member, who said that after three failed rounds of marriage therapy she felt like her husband was a roommate. Thirty-two-year-old Don, also unhappily married, wanted to show off his physique but not his face so he posed in his jockey shorts in front of a full length mirror and shot his own photo in such a way that the flash created a big starburst that eclipsed everything from the neck up. Plenty of other dating sites like Matchmaker, Lavalife and Date.com also accept married members, saying they are not in the business of making a moral judgment on extramarital affairs.

Rather, theirs is a business of collecting membership fees, and they can expand their potential audience by welcoming the unhappily married along with the unhappily single. "It doesn't surprise me," said Matthew Harrington, an analyst who follows USA Interactive for the investment bank Janco Partners. "Given primate behavior, it creates a larger market for them." There is a flip side to that argument, that singles who are serious about finding a life partner may be less likely to visit sites patronized by married folks. That is the reasoning used by Match.com and Yahoo Personals, and it seems to have some merit. The two biggest American dating sites are arguably two of the most moralistic. However, when Interactive Inc. decided to expand its online dating empire through an acquisition, it selected something a little spicier than Match.com, thereby capturing both sides of the online dating spectrum. While Match.com insists that people at least maintain the pretense of

being interested in a well-rounded relationship and rejects memberships from people who say they are joining purely for sex, uDate
seems to encourage the pursuit of no-strings-attached relationships.
Under the question, "What do you really want from joining
uDate?" members may check pen pals, friendship, romance, relationship, fun, sex or marriage. In fact, the whole flavor of the
uDate membership application seems to invite those interested in
something less than wholesome. One question, "Do you take
drugs?" offers these choices of responses:

- Not Specified
- I don't take drugs
- I've given up taking drugs
- I want to give up
- I occasionally take drugs
- I enjoy it
- I love it
- I take drugs to excess!!

Other questions on the membership form take a similar tone.
One asks, "When it comes to sex, are you adventurous?" and
offers the following choices:

- Not Specified
- Not Really
- It Depends
- Quite Adventurous
- Very Adventurous
- Anything Goes!!

It is not simply the larger potential customer base uDate wins by
opening its membership to habitual drug-users, sexual thrill-seekers

and the not-so-happily married. Unlike the straight-and-narrow singles who want nothing more than to find a June or Ward Cleaver so they can be done with dating for good, those stuck in unhappy marriages may be more likely to keep coming back for more. The not-so-happily married who, for one reason or another, plan to stay married, tend to describe their existence as a kind of limbo of discontent from which they can only manage temporary, albeit repeated, escapes. In fact, the inability of much of this population to make a decisive change in their lives makes them good steady customers in the online dating business, an industry that all too often loses its best customers when wedding bells ring.

It is easy enough to conclude that the Internet facilitates cheating; the extent to which it does so, over and over again, may not be fully understood by anyone who does not partake. Ted is a 40-year-old salesman from Dallas who did not know what to expect when he signed up for a small online dating service that accepted memberships from married people. "My life is fine, I love my wife and I have everything I want," he said. "I guess I am just curious about other ladies." It was in October that Ted posted his first-ever Internet ad, saying he was seeking "a special friend who doesn't mind the fact that I'm married." Almost immediately, he heard from several women, and two weeks later, for the first time in 10 years of married monogamy, he kissed another woman. "I ate a whole pack of antacid, and was still about sick," he said of his nerves leading up to that encounter. Afterward, he was giddy with excitement, and eagerly looking forward to another adventure.

Ted's story is typical for the way the Internet may speed the conversion from cheating mind to first-time cheater and then to habitual cheater. Once he discovered how easy, how risk-free it was to make discreet connections online, he quickly went back for more. His job in sales kept him on the road frequently with a schedule that was vague enough that he could mix business and pleasure trips without his wife questioning why he was away. He set up an anonymous email account and conducted all his correspondence at Kinko's. Two weeks after his first extramarital kiss, Ted had found two more women through the dating site. He arranged to meet them at hotels about 50 miles out of town. By December, his extra-marital dalliances had become weekly events. Sometimes he managed to squeeze in two during a single Saturday. Ted said he had no desire to leave his wife; he just wasn't happy with their sex life anymore. She had just been promoted to a much more demanding job and was spending a lot of time with an old college friend who had recently moved to town. He swore she was so busy herself that she did not even notice he was away more often. Ted also had no interest in a steady girlfriend. He wanted quick, intense encounters, and his online dating service kept a steady supply of women who were looking for the same. One time, an unmarried woman responded to his ad. She saw him a couple of times but confessed that she was really after a long-term relationship with an unmarried man. When she found what she was looking for, she gave Ted the number of a married friend whose motives were more in line with his. "Just like so many people, her friend is married and content, just wants to have sex again, like me and everyone else. It's kind of a niche, I guess," Ted said. By Christmas, Ted could not get over the way his life had changed. "It is like I am a kid again," he said. "I probably don't sound like a very nice guy, but it's strange. I am having more sex with more women now than I ever did when I was single."

Most marriage therapists are accustomed to hearing about infidelity and many say that after years of practice they doubt whether monogamy is a realistic goal for all people. So they are not simply speaking from a high moral perch when they say they are troubled by the way the Internet makes it so much easier to cheat. "The Internet is like a microwave for sex. It makes you braver and stupider," said Karen Ross, a marriage and family therapist in Chicago. Although technology is not to blame for the fundamental challenges all couples face trying to stay engaged in their marriages, Ross said the difference with the Internet is the abundance of willing partners it provides. Infidelity may sometimes be inevitable when marriages or long-term partnerships are unraveling, she said, but other couples are better off just riding out the lulls that are a normal part of any relationship.

Others are more interested in the way all the increased access seems to be weakening long-standing taboos, or at least stated taboos, about infidelity. Al Cooper, head of the Marital and Sexuality Centre in San Jose, California, and author of two clinical psychology books about the connection between sex and the Internet, says that in the same way people with all kinds of bizarre sexual fetishes have found communities online, so too are the unhappily married, perhaps even the happily married but restless, made to understand that they are not alone. "Particularly around sexual issues and accompanying concerns of normalcy, finding others who share the same interest may facilitate acceptance," said Cooper.

Dan Savage, who writes a nationally syndicated sex advice column and has become an outspoken advocate of letting consenting adults do as they please, says there is no debating that the Internet facilitates infidelity. "It allows you to find someone in the same city where you live, who you would otherwise never cross paths with. It also allows someone who may be casually thinking about cheating to dabble." But Savage argues that this is not necessarily a bad thing. He believes people are monogamous to different degrees, and a marriage between two not-so-monogamous people can be a good match, provided they can both find extra-marital partners. He also maintains that a marriage is not necessarily over when a couple stops having sex, and for people in this situation, such as those caring for a very ill spouse, a discreet affair may actually help them sustain the marriage. "Some people believe their marriages should be intense sexual carnivals, but that is not always the case," says

Savage. "I think our attitude toward infidelity is gradually moving toward the attitude you see more often in Europe. It happens."

You could say that Internet dating was what ended the marriage of Stuart, a 41-year-old accountant living outside of St. Louis, Missouri, but today neither he nor his ex-wife has any regrets. Married for 15 years, Stuart endured a slow and painful process of understanding his own homosexuality and then mustering up the nerve to confront it. He was in his mid-thirties when he began struggling with a depression that led him to seek counseling and ultimately come out of the closet. Today he is divorced and happily involved with a man he met through friends, but he says he honestly does not know if his life would have turned out this way had he not had online chat rooms and dating sites, where he could mingle anonymously. "For many gay men, the Internet is very important," Stuart said. "Many of them are married, or they are just in the closet and afraid to go out and make it known they are gay. I would have been terrified to go into a gay bar and talk to anyone."

On sites like Date.com, which keep out of their members' business, you can find a lot of ads like this one posted by a 50-year-old man from the Midwest, who stated up front that he smoked, was a little chubby and had a wife. "I'll tell it like it is," he wrote. "I'm married and intend to stay that way. I'm not looking for a soul mate, the love of my life, or someone to grow old with. I'm just looking for someone like me who is a little bored with the same ol' same ol.' If you would like to forget who you are for a little while, break the boredom, and have a little no-strings-attached fun, get in touch. I don't care what you look like." Such a posting would never make it to publication on Match.com or Yahoo, but many people believe married people are present in volumes on those sites too, the only difference being that they keep their status secret. Even the sites that say they do not admit married people typically do allow separated people to join, basically providing for a huge amount of wiggle room. When asked for its definition, Match.com maintains that separated means not living under the same roof with your spouse. Some of its members, though, define that more liberally, such as not living under the same roof while traveling on business. Several women who have joined one of the "for singles only" dating sites say they have heard from married men, often men from different cities who suggest they arrange to meet while they are in town on business. There is one widely circulated estimate that suggests 30 percent of the people on American dating sites are married, but that figure, which originally came from the Internet industry research firm Jupiter Research, seems to be more of an educated guess than anything else. Because of all the different policies of different dating sites and the people who simply lie about their status, getting a good number would seem impossible. Still, the logic of married people joining such sites seems undeniable. Much of what has been said about the convenience of online dating for single people, after all, would seem to be twice as appealing for married people. Finding dates on the Internet, especially for those who are not too discerning, is fast, and it is private.

One of the most popular dating destinations for residents of the greater San Francisco Bay Area is Craig's List, a general community site for posting résumés, apartment vacancies, as well as personal ads. The free personals section of Craig's List is one of the site's main draws, and within that site, a section called Casual Encounters lets people candidly advertise for quick sexual encounters. While that site features many postings from single people thinking no further than the evening before them, it also attracts volumes of married people looking for discreet affairs and couples seeking threesomes. On a recent Sunday this one Web site serving the greater San Francisco area had 50 ads from married people, like this one: "MARRIED MAN, BORED, SEEKS FIRST AFFAIR. I need to know if I can still enjoy sex...will you help me?" Craig Newmark, the founder and chairman of Craig's List, maintains that his site is simply fulfilling a need and not creating one. "As long as they are taking responsibility for their own actions, that's OK with me," Newmark said. "Our business is to help out with people's everyday needs, whether that means sex or stamp collecting." If Craig's List is any indication of the rest of the online dating world, then the ratio of short-term thrill seekers to long-term relationship seekers is high. Newmark said that in one recent week his site ran 18,000 personal ads, 8,000 of which were in the "casual encounters" section.

11

THE LOVE BUNKER

"I am extremely sick of the bar scene, yet I am a bouncer, go figure. I guess that is why I am putting up this profile."

—A 25-year-old New York man

Casual dress and scooters in the workplace, not to mention company executives under the age of 40, were supposed to have gone out years ago with the Internet bust, but in a little office in Richardson, Texas, everyone is still partying like it's 1999. The Match.com office, a wide-open floor of cubicle workstations with scooters propped up against the wall, looks a lot like all the other dotcom companies that thrived in San Francisco's warehouse district years ago. The vibe feels the same too, as Melanie Angermann, Match.com's 41-year-old director of advertising, surveys the scene and sighs that she must be the oldest person on staff. Chief Executive Tim Sullivan is still several months shy of his 40th birthday. For the most part, the office is full of very young employees who buzz about with a sense of

137

Serious talk about removing the stigma of online dating at the Match.com headquarters. Reuters.

urgency and boundless optimism. Even the customer service grunts say they love their jobs. No one talks much about how big the company has become, how it has become synonymous with the entire phenomenon of online dating. Like good entrepreneurs, they are focused firmly on the future, on all the room they still have to grow, and as they outline their ambitious vision, old buzzwords of what used to be the New Economy keep cropping up. "Our business model provides great economies of scale," says the company's chief technology officer, Mike Presz. "Think of all the bars you'd have to go into to meet the people we could provide you in 20 minutes." The national economy remained depressed, but at Match.com, right off the President George Bush Turnpike, no one was talking about cutbacks. They were spending like crazy on advertising to get the message out to the still-unconverted, while racing to forge hundreds of seemingly random business partnerships—the kind that were also fashionable back in 1999—

with companies with which you would think they shared nothing in common other than an Internet presence.

The weather was on a lot of people's minds one morning in early December as an ice storm swept the eastern United States. The storm had brought nothing more than an unusual chill to Dallas, but everyone knew that was likely to produce many new Match.com memberships. Weather.com is just one of the many sites where Match.com advertises, and some people who went online that day, worried only about the pipes freezing in their homes or ice slowing their commute to work, would surely see that Match.com banner and click on through. It might not be the most intuitive partnership—a weather site and a dating site—but when you thought about it, it wasn't just married people who tracked snowstorms. One of the benefits of having an eight-million-member database is that Match.com can track all sorts of details about its customers: how they landed on its site in the first place, what they want in a mate, how often they typically email before arranging to meet. The company can crunch the numbers on random things, like how far people in different regions of the United States will travel for a date (women in Chicago and men in New York City are the laziest), or where red-headed women are the most desirable (San Antonio, Texas). It says smokers have the worst odds of getting a date in Honolulu, while men with tattoos will do best in Allentown, Pennsylvania. If men under 5'8" find themselves losing out to taller guys, they might consider relocating to Syracuse, New York, where, more than any other region of the country, the women say they like short men. Match.com says the facts it has collected even contradict that age-old wisdom that gentlemen prefer blondes. Gentlemen who subscribe to Match.com prefer women with light brown hair.

There are other fun aspects to working at a dating business: as a site that strives to keep its content clean and keep married people away, Match.com requires that every single profile and photo submitted be screened by someone on staff before it is published. Including the word "married" in your profile is the surest way to be rejected (although sometimes married folks do sneak through), but the company is pretty strict about photos as well. No nudity, no excessive cleavage and no pictures shot in thong bikinis, unless the person can figure out a way to keep her face in the photo too. No one has figured out how to do that yet. To the amusement of the Match.com staff, many singles post photos of themselves with an unidentified arm around their shoulders. Then there are the bogus photos. Some members have been known to post pictures of people they think are more attractive than themselves, and some have had the audacity to scan magazine photos of minor celebrities, like an actor from India or a diver from Sweden. The unknowing customer service staff lets the pictures through, but then another member notices the fraud. Once, a particularly curious request came in that the site take down an "inappropriate" photo posted by a male member. The staff was stumped. It was a perfectly decent photo of a guy sitting, with his hands folded in front of him. Or was it? They took a closer look. Some thought that perhaps he was exposing himself, but it was almost impossible to say for sure, with his hands in the way and the shadows in the picture. There were four customer support people huddled around a computer screen trying to decipher it. "We were like, 'OK there is one finger, and there is his thumb, but what is *that?*'" recalls Gwen Reich, the company's customer care manager.

Reich has also trained her staff to spot red flags in the text people write to accompany photos. You can't post a profile saying you are looking for a roll in the hay, unless you add that you also like to play the piano or surf or go dancing. This is the vague rule of thumb Match.com applies to help keep its service from being strictly a sex site. It's OK to say you like sex, as long as you make clear it's in the context of a well-rounded relationship full of other non-sexual recreational activities. Still, these rules are more than a little bit fuzzy, and the customer service team has shared many a laugh trying to figure out if someone is attempting to skirt the rules or just looking for some innocent fun. "If a person is talking about water sports they better be mentioning a lake or a jet ski," Reich deadpans. Other than that, it tends to let people present themselves as they are, warts and all. It declines, for example, to use its spell-check function to clean up member profiles, reasoning that if someone uses bad grammar or can't spell, their dates should know.

Collectively, though, the profiles are bland more often than they are intriguing. "'I can't believe I'm doing this,'" one Match.com staffer says with a roll of her eyes, referring to what could be the phrase people use most often to introduce themselves. A lot of the people who join Match.com seem to think they are the only ones who are uneasy with the idea of launching such a public search for love. They feel a need to apologize, or acknowledge their discomfort from the start. "'My friends made me do this,'" another Match.com staffer chimes in, while a third adds, "'We'll have to make up a story about where we met.'" Before they even have met anyone online, these self-conscious members have an alternative story all ready to go. But the biggest yawn of all: "'Tired of the bar scene.'" Sometimes it seems as if every other person on Match.com has joined because they are tired of the bar scene, or simply can't think of a better opening line. Judging from the profiles posted on Match.com, the bar scene is looking tired everywhere, from Tampa, Florida, to St. Louis, Missouri, Portland, Oregon, and Lincoln, Nebraska. On the other hand, moonlit walks on the beach are popular nationwide. You would never know that much of the country is landlocked judging from how many Match.com members, hailing from places like Wyoming, list moonlit walks on the beach as their number-one pastime. Some seasoned Match.com members have even begun addressing this lack of originality. "Why does it seem that everyone on this system seems to either roller blade, ski, hike, or take long slow walks on the beach," one San

Francisco man wrote in his own profile. "Where are all these supposed beach walkers when I go to Ocean Beach?"

Originality may be lacking. On the other hand, Match.com does not think a herd mentality is all bad. As it tried to blow the roof off its still relatively small base of paid subscribers at the end of 2002, it was striving to craft an image of its service as something that everyone knows about, talks about and, if they are single, uses. "We are still at the tip of the iceberg of awareness and legitimacy," said Chief Executive Sullivan. At Match.com, people often share stories of how they got into the business, how their spouses wrinkled their noses and said it sounded suspiciously like a porn business or how their mothers warned them that it might not look so good on their résumés. Sullivan said he faced no such resistance from anyone in his inner circle. Although he had been married for years when he first entered the industry, he says he always had a great empathy for single people and believed matchmaking was "a business poised for great growth." He estimates that today somewhere between one million and two million Americans pay to subscribe to an online dating service, but believes that number can become many times larger relatively soon. "I'm incredibly optimistic that awareness is not what it will be in 12 months," he suggests, noting that the company is focused on removing the stigma that has long dogged newspaper personals and Internet chat rooms. That stigma, though, is strangely persistent, even within the Match.com offices. On the one hand, Sullivan goes on about online dating being an obvious move for singles. Yet he admits that he would rather keep out of print the name of a family member who used Match.com, out of respect for that person's privacy.

Stigma is what keeps Melanie Angermann up at night. When customers are not willing evangelists, it makes her job of promoting the company that much harder. The sense of embarrassment over using an online dating site is still so pervasive that *The Wall Street Journal*, not long before it pronounced online dating one of the hot new trends, published an article about all the people who told lies about meeting their significant others through friends rather than admitting they had used the Internet. If competition from the likes of Yahoo Personals is stiff, Match maintains that the biggest competition of all is the complacency, or shame, that might keep singles offline altogether. For years the company ran humorous ads that sought to knock down the fairy-tale notion that love was something that just floated into your life and not something you went searching for. One such spot featured a character named Destiny. He was characterized as a sloppy slacker who lounged around in his bathrobe watching TV and let the answering machine pick up when people called. As Match.com unveiled its aggressive new ad campaign for 2003, it went a step further. A series of new television commercials featured couples in serious romantic settings—a church wedding or that first dinner with the parents— where they soberly announced they had serious confessions to make, and then, somewhat anticlimactically, revealed that they had met on Match.com.

From the outside, as 2002 drew to a close, online dating was bigger than ever, and it might have seemed that Match.com was riding the momentum of so much buzz. But in meetings at the company's main conference room, a bright-red, oval-shaped structure called the Love Bunker, executives were spending a lot of time talking about stigma. "You can sit here and say, 'I think online dating makes sense for some people but it's not for me,'" says Angermann. "I want to break down the 'not for me' part. The number-one goal is to help eradicate that stigma." To that end, Angermann generously goes beyond the call of professional duty, volunteering that she is not just a Match.com employee, but she is also a customer, or rather a user, since free Match.com membership is the perk that comes with the job. A pretty and vivacious blonde, Angermann says she is looking for a man who likes big dogs, good red wines and challenging discussions. Her one pet peeve? No mustaches, please. In other cases the online dating perk works the other way around; a job at Match.com comes with a Match.com membership. David Draughon was between jobs three years ago when he met his future wife, Rebecca, through Match.com. Rebecca was a Match.com product manager and as the relationship grew, she referred David to a position in the company's quality control division, where he has worked ever since.

One place where you might think the stigma of online dating has been all but eradicated is in California's Silicon Valley, a region where computer proficiency could be the highest in the world, where people are quick to try all kinds of new technologies, and where locals complain the high ratio of men to women makes it hard to find love through traditional social channels. The region has earned another stereotype, as a place populated by engineers who log long hours in the office, lack basic social skills and tend to use computer-enabled communication as a crutch to avoid the scarier face-to-face interaction.

It is a bone-chilling Friday night in December in Sunnyvale, California, right in the center of Silicon Valley, and the rain is coming down in sheets. It is the kind of weather that would make any lonely single, and not just a socially inept single, want to stay home and surf the Net. But stereotypes can lie. Inclement weather notwithstanding, residents of this supposedly antisocial town are out in force. Men and women, but mostly men, are mingling in small groups at all the bars in town. Several tables are occupied by groups of four or five men who really don't even have to concern themselves with working up the nerve to approach a woman. There are simply not enough women to go around. So why should the men go to the bar at all when there are photos of hundreds of women from their very zip code posted on sites like Match.com?

The suggestion of Internet dating draws chuckles and knowing smiles from a group of three work buddies. They have certainly heard of Internet dating and they have friends who have tried it.

But even for this technology-savvy, socially isolated population, there remains a wide gulf between thinking about it and actually doing it. Even in Silicon Valley, the stigma remains. "You would assume that only the most desperate people do that," says John, a 35-year-old manager at a software company, who confesses that he has no firsthand knowledge of what kind of people are online, since he is happily married. His two friends are single, but one is either too shy or too embarrassed by the suggestion of dating to even offer his thoughts. He sits and doodles on a piece of paper while the third friend, Lloyd, explains why he still hasn't signed up.

Lloyd is a 33-year-old engineer with a scruffy beard and a wiry frame he says is the result of a month on the Atkins Diet. He says he has had enough adventure for a lifetime and now is "dying" to find the right woman and settle down in a white picket fence sort of life. Lloyd has recently returned home after several years living abroad in Europe and Asia, and he admits that while he loves his job and the opportunities to travel it has brought him, it has also cost him a number of relationships. Sure, he knows about online dating. He has visited some sites and "came this close" to signing up, he says, pinching his fingers together. A number of times, he has even started filling out the registration form, his age, his hair color, and then...Lloyd can never complete the process. When he is asked to write a short paragraph about himself, he is stumped. "I feel stupid explaining myself," he says.

At that, John, his married friend, offers that this is the problem with online dating. That no one really knows how to sell themselves. For John, love has nothing to do with any of the information people are asked to provide when they join an online dating service. He and his wife, he says, have few shared interests. "To me, it's all about chemistry, and that doesn't come across online. The grin, the extended look, all those subtleties that really engage you."

Once again, the group returns to the other problem with online dating. "There is a negative stigma," insists Lloyd. "That it's just for really desperate men and women." A woman joins the table and shares the group's sentiments. She too, is unattached and finding it difficult to meet men. She too has dabbled with online dating, going so far as to cruise through the profiles and even correspond with a number of men. But like Lloyd, she hasn't been able to bring herself to post her own profile. "I don't know," she says, her body reshaping into a mild cringe. "I just can never go through with it." When one of the men at the table brings up the stigma factor yet again, she nods knowingly. "There was this one filmmaker I was corresponding with," she muses. "He was really delightful. We were getting ready to meet and then he wrote to me and told me he had met someone else at a party. He found someone offline. I guess all the good ones do."

Lloyd is still wondering how he would ever get beyond the personal profile part of the application. He rolls his eyes, imagining the self-portrait he would offer. "I am an outdoorsy kind of guy," he says, rolling his eyes. "I love to fish, I love to ski, I treat myself well...Hell, it's difficult to write about yourself. I'll tell you what I really want. I want Mrs. Cleaver. "But it's hard to say I want a homemaker."

Another group of single men grapples with the same dilemma. They are certainly not meeting any women at this bar, and they say the pickings are even slimmer at work. But they are not running home and signing up for an online dating service either. "I've looked at the Web site, and there's a hurdle there," says Scott, a chubby blond guy in khakis and a polo shirt. "I don't meet a lot of women, but I also have never heard of anyone who said, 'I went online and now I'm dating this girl.'" He pauses. "Except there was this friend of mine... Oh, maybe I'll get around to doing it."

Lloyd, too, is thinking more and more about doing it, as he reflects on his last love. "My old girlfriend used to go out with me in the first snow and climb up the mountain. We'd dig a snow cave and spend the night there and then we'd ski down in the morning," he recalls wistfully.

His friend John breaks the mood with a loud laugh. "June Cleaver in snow shoes," he laughs. "That's what you want."

"I suppose I do," says Lloyd. "But I don't know how many women would respond to that ad."

It is the Lloyds and the Scotts of the world, single yet squeamish about Internet dating, that Match.com is seeking to reach through its advertising. "We think advertising is critical," Chief Executive Sullivan reiterated, months later, after he had just survived the Valentine's Day crush, what Christmas time is to the retail industry. "It is critical to converting the non-early adopters, to show them that online dating is a mainstream concept that is worth trying. In just the past few months," Sullivan says, "the momentum seems to have accelerated." During the Valentine's Day season, he said he was struck not by how many newspapers and television shows did segments on online dating, but by how they treated the topic so matter-of-factly. "The tone was different," he said.

"It was not so much 'online dating is a big business now isn't that cute,' as it was 'this is a really important change in the way people are meeting and interacting.'"

When a satisfied online dating customer decides to go public, it seems to have a lot more impact than any paid ad. Increasingly, newspaper wedding announcements mention Match.com or other dating sites. A June 2002 announcement in the high-profile *New York Times* wedding section cited Match.com as the force that ultimately brought together 37-year-old Hilary Haika Glazer and 44-year-old Craig Bromberg. The couple did not initially meet through Match.com. Rather, Bromberg noticed Glazer while she was singing at Rosh Hashanah services at her synagogue, but was too shy to approach her. He waited a full year to see her again at Rosh Hashanah services, where he then worked up the courage—to ask a friend to introduce them. It didn't work. Glazer said she had had a series of bad blind dates and was not interested in any more. But she was more open-minded than she let on. Weeks later, Bromberg discovered her photo on Match.com, and that time when he reached out to her, she responded. Such stories are beginning to pile up. When Match.com launched in 1995, it took nearly a year for it to sign up 60,000 members. Today it signs up that many every few days.

As a company that is rapidly increasing both its subscriber and its revenue base (revenues more than doubled in the fourth quarter of 2002 to $37 million), Match.com continues its struggle to be taken seriously. Tim Sullivan is frequently interviewed on television, and he always looks forward to the opportunity to discuss an Internet business model that actually works. Instead, he is often asked about silly stuff, such as tips on flirting. Such is the territory when your business is love. Today, however, Match.com is in the process of expanding its enterprise beyond online dating, exploring the places that voice and video and wireless technology, as well as its vast consumer database, might lead it. This company, which may have done more than any other to get people to stay in and look for mates on the computer, now is branching out into an events business, hosting parties, wine tastings, singles dinners and even adventure travel and cruises to get people to mingle the old-fashioned way. Although online dating is the company's bread and butter, today it says it is in the business of connecting people in whatever way works. "I think online dating has probably softened people up to other kinds of dating events," says Chris Terrell, head of Match.com's special-events business. Although the company has not yet exploited all the possibilities, the potential of combining its offline events business with its eight-million-member online database are enticing, suggesting a way of gathering people who have much more in common than just the sorry fact of being single. "Say there was a way to get people who had 80 percent in common together in one room," suggests Terrell.

The company also is exploring ways to help its members reveal more about their character and is playing around with its own psychological tests that it might eventually incorporate into the registration process. "Chemistry can somewhat be bottled," argues Sullivan. "Personally, I think it can be. We are analyzing how people reach the qualities they find attractive. We, as a technology company, can provide filtering, sorting, and searching tools." Currently, the only search tools Match.com can enable, while vast in scope, are relatively superficial. Members may search by age, location, physical characteristics or hobbies, such as the mention of mountain biking in a profile. Sullivan says he envisions a day when many more subtle questions could be incorporated. "Instead of asking, 'are you shy,' we could ask 'how do you feel when you walk into a crowded room full of strangers?'"

There are other ways as well that the site might easily be enhanced, but they are more controversial. For a business that is so often compared with eBay, Match.com and online dating sites in general have consistently failed to adopt one key component of the online auction model: the feedback system. When you buy or sell something on eBay, users may rate you. The way such a system might work in the online dating world are intriguing: "She has more than 'a few extra pounds.'" "His photo must have been taken five years ago, before he lost all his hair." Sullivan winces to talk about this, knowing that a feedback system is a dicey proposal. What the company might gain by providing more truthful information to some members, it would probably lose again by alienating many others who are fearful of having their looks or their first date manners debated so publicly. Besides, it could be that the company's biggest strength is not advanced psychological profiling or sorting technology so much as it is the sheer power of its numbers. Although not everybody who joins Match.com attracts volumes of suitors, those who are young and attractive and live in big cities can attract them at a rate that would be virtually impossible to duplicate anywhere else. On Valentine's Day 2003, Jennifer Georges became something of a Match.com prom queen when her profile was viewed more than any other member on the system. Georges, a 28-year-old brunette from New York, who boasted that she knew how to milk a cow and was not one of those "vacuous waif-type" women, had her Match.com profile read by 4,462 people on February 14 alone.

12

BEYOND THE LAPTOP

"I am looking to go all the way for my first time tonight. I want to do whatever you want me to do RIGHT NOW!!!!"

—A 22-year-old Oregon man

Long before millions of people began clicking over the Internet, there were at least several thousand who were meeting through telephone and video dating services. Today the online dating industry is trying to enhance the way singles can present themselves by incorporating some of those older technologies onto their Web sites. On many of the largest sites like Yahoo Personals, for instance, singles can now use their telephones to record a voice message that accompanies their print ads, or, if they have webcams, shoot some video of themselves. Combine the webcam with Yahoo's instant messenger and, voilà, they can converse and see each other in real time. "It makes the overall experience better," said Samantha Lazear, senior product manager for Yahoo Personals. "One guy sang a song

151

that he wrote. It just made him so much more endearing. It tells you more." Yahoo has found that people who post photos to accompany text profiles receive eight times as many responses, and it hopes that by incorporating voice and video it will improve the odds that much more, making online dating not just a more realistic experience, but a more productive one.

Other companies are focusing on different technologies to improve what are still too often slim odds of getting a response. A company called SMS.ac, which offers a service for people to send and receive text messages from their mobile phones and other wireless devices, has discovered that a large portion of its ten million customers around the world are using its service to date or at least do some innocent flirting. Recently, it launched smsFlirt, a text messaging service directed at those romance-minded customers. People from 170 countries are using it. SMS basically works like the "old" Internet dating services, letting people search by age, location, hair color or hobbies and then fire off a message to the names the search engine produces. There is one big difference: Messages sent from cell phones are much more likely to reach the recipients in real time. Michael Pousti, who cofounded SMS.ac in 2001 and now serves as its chief executive, argues that shifting the dating technology from a personal computer to a cellular phone could improve the response rate by a staggering 100 percent. His logic? Pousti had previously worked at a community Web site for college students where he found that only about 1 percent of the community's members was online at any given time. To get from 1 percent to 100 percent would assume that cellular users never sleep, bathe, go to movies, ride airplanes or become otherwise indisposed. Still, it is easy to conceive of a dramatically improved response rate if you can reach people while they are out and about.

Middle-aged people like John Burson, who grew up when newspaper personals were just coming into vogue, might marvel at the fast pace of Internet dating. But younger people, and others who are not all that young but just love gadgets, are increasingly regarding Internet dating as slow and old, and oddly formal. Brad Ricks is a software salesman from Yuma, Arizona, who has played around on some of the big dating sites, but always felt a little uncomfortable with how finding a serious mate was the stated goal from the outset. More often now, he connects with new people through his cell phone, using SMS. In addition to preferring the more immediate contact this allows, he likes the casual tone of wireless messaging better. Since Ricks frequently travels for work, he will use SMS to locate people in cities where he has business trips scheduled. Although most of his travel is confined to the United States, he could—if he wanted to—find people to chat with in Bolivia, Iceland, even Romania, which is one of SMS's top five markets. Today, the size of the SMS customer base in the United States lags behind a number of countries, including Indonesia, Malaysia, Britain and Romania, but it is rapidly catching up. Wherever he has traveled in the United States, Ricks has never had trouble finding someone to talk to.

He says he often has no expectation other than to make contact with someone who can send him the local weather details or restaurant recommendations. If he happens to make contact with a woman, and the exchange goes well, then he might make plans to meet her. He finds this wireless technology gets much closer than computer-based Internet dating to replicating traditional ways of mingling, where people would meet in the course of their everyday lives, and decide gradually, based on the quality of the connection, whether they wished to pursue a friendship or more. When you send casual "hi, how are you, how's the weather" messages from a mobile phone, Ricks argues, the pressure is off. People don't sweat it much if they don't get a response, although usually they do. He has used SMS to connect with several people, and he has met a few, including one woman from across the country whom he liked quite a bit, but chose not to pursue because of the distance. "I've also used Match.com and some of the others, and they seem real formal," he said. "This suits my needs much better. I am 28, and not necessarily looking to settle down just yet. This is more of an informational message service, a community. It is a bunch of buddies who help you out."

The big dating services, too, have caught on to the benefits of wireless dating and several have their own services up and running, or sketched out on the drawing board. Increasingly, when you launch your search for a date from a wireless device, you will be able to scan not only by city and zip code, but by your exact location at a given moment, thanks to global positioning technologies that make it possible to determine the latitude and longitude of a person using a cell phone. Such technologies, rapidly being implemented in the United States and elsewhere, are often regarded as an important tool for 911 operators and police tracking criminals and missing persons. But the dating industry sees a benefit too.

Global positioning is still somewhat spotty in the United States, but in places where this location technology is working well, stories are already appearing of people who made last-minute searches for a date and found one. Moviso, a company that makes technology for transmitting wireless content, recently went into partnership with Match.com to make its service available from cell phones. Moviso President Shawn Conahan argues that the way people are using these services already suggests an evolution of the whole notion of what it means to date. Because you can launch a search from a precise geographic location at any given time, whether it be your home, the beach, a coffee shop or a hotel in a strange city, there is a strong tendency toward last-minute meetings. Recently, Conahan and a group of male colleagues attending a trade show in Las Vegas tried to get into a nightclub when a bouncer who was keeping the male/female ratio in balance blocked them at the door. For a man to be granted entry, he had to be accompanied by a woman. Although Conahan and his friends knew no women in the immediate vicinity, he assumed there were other all-female groups in the line outside the club who would confront the same problem. "Using this dating application, we could have just pinged someone within the general radius." Even before online dating went wireless, there was no shortage of "hook up for sex" sites serving people who had something other than dinner and a movie on their minds. Place this bold approach to casual sex on a cellular phone, and the potential for even more very-last-minute hookups seems almost mind-boggling. "Dating, as it turns out, is a gray area," said Conahan.

Match.com has never sought to be in that business of quick hookups, but like so many other dating services, it believes all the new technology it is adopting will serve the conservative and cautious as much as it serves the risk takers and thrill seekers. For instance, those who still prefer using phones the old fashioned way—to talk—are the target of another new Match.com service that arranges phone dates. Instead of just picking up the phone and dialing the number of someone they meet on the site, Match.com members can schedule a phone date through the Web site, decide on a time and then have an operator connect them, the same way a conference call operator does for businesses.

Is this a high-tech solution to a problem that never really existed in the first place? Not at all argues Match.com, which says the phone date service addresses the security concerns of many people, particularly women, who are not comfortable giving out their phone numbers, yet are just as unwilling to take the initiative of calling a strange man. When the phone call is arranged like a conference call, those cautious women can retain a passive role of waiting for the phone to ring, while at the same time preserving their sense of security.

Voice, video and wireless are in many ways the most obvious ways to advance a business that has its roots in technology, but at the same time the industry is exploiting the lower-tech, traditional ways of dating too. Match.com's offline events, often attended by people who still swear they would never look for a date online, are drawing large crowds. Around the same time Internet dating started showing hockey stick growth and universal recognition, Match.com began venturing into live events in New York and Los Angeles, and continued rapidly expanding from there. Today, residents of San Francisco can keep themselves almost as busy as Match.com's online members by attending a ballroom dancing event, a gourmet cooking class, a cocktail party, a sit-down dinner, a movie screening and much, much, more as they say, all in a single month.

Does anyone have an excuse anymore for staying home on a Saturday night?

As dating services of all kinds grow, it seems more and more odd that anyone would be so passive as to simply live their life and wait for love to come into it. Even though it may still be struggling to convert large blocks of single people, the online dating industry already seems to have created a whole new way of dating. Paradoxically, the shift has people taking matters of the heart a little less seriously, even as they are more upfront than ever about their quest for love, sex, companionship, or as the case may be, just a handyman. Jennifer Georges, the long-haired brunette from New York who was viewed more than any other Match.com member on Valentine's Day 2003, often follows a rigorous dating schedule that once upon a time might have been difficult for even a beauty queen to aspire to. When she is not attached to one single man, Georges says she will sometimes go out on three different dates with three different men in a single week. If someone like Georges were to make a New Year's resolution not to be single by Valentine's Day, her goal would not seem at all unrealistic; she might easily have 30 men to review in that narrow time frame. Georges, who left a marketing job on Wall Street to work for a family business, says she has had a lot of fun in her life and would now like to be in an exclusive relationship. But that is not the reason for all this activity. "I am definitely ready to be committed to one person...but I also like to go out and I like to see what there is in the city. If someone wants to get together with me, I trust in myself that my time is not going to be wasted. My dates are not necessarily all romantic dates." They are not all Starbucks quickies either. Some of the men Georges has met online have taken her out to dinner and to the theater on their first date.

Leave it to Match.com, then, to declare it acceptable, even a good thing, to date more than one person at a time. The company recently came up with the term "hyper-romance" to describe the trend of a casual dating practice that is "all about having fun and enjoying dates with new and interesting people," and a "great way to build relationship skills" to boot. Match.com even issued a tip sheet for successful hyper-dating, advising singles that something it termed "date crossover" was to be avoided. "It's tacky to discuss other people you're dating with your date du jour. Avoid situations where you may run into, or end up socializing, with more than one romantic interest at a time, and don't repeat last night's date (same restaurant, nightclub, movie) with tonight's romantic interest," the tip sheet said. Not surprisingly, Match.com's survey of its own members found that the younger the singles were, the more likely they were to engage in hyper-romance.

In this trend, too, there is a strong parallel in the offline dating scene, particularly in one recent phenomenon known as speed dating. These ultra-hyper-dating events gather an equal number of men and women and sit them down in a line of tables or some other formation that enables the men to rotate chairs every five, six or eight minutes. Speed dating, which is popular in most big urban areas and has been widely discussed in the media, seems to owe its success both to the popularity of Internet dating and the backlash against it. Once people became OK about saying they were ready to turn to a dating service, some also came to dislike the anonymity of Internet dating, where email flirtations could go on indefinitely. "I think people are very frustrated with other methods of dating that are time consuming," said Tom Jaffe, who founded and now runs 8MinuteDating.com, one of the major speed dating companies in the country. "What is really important," Jaffe argues, "is meeting in person, that first moment." Depending on whether you have a sense of humor about it, speed dating may sound more than a little callous. Sponsors even encourage you to take notes during the event so that when you go home you can remember whether Joe was the one who made you laugh, the one who gave you a soggy handshake or the one who had you looking at your watch. But efficiency is the whole point. "If eight minutes seems like a long time with somebody, then you probably don't want to spend a whole evening with them," says Jaffe.

Speed dating works a little differently depending on who has organized the event, but typically people are discouraged from sharing very personal information or phone numbers then and there. Instead, when they go home, they can log onto a Web site and check those names of people with whom they felt a possible attraction. (You can't always say for sure after eight minutes.) If your crushes check your name too, then both of you are notified by email of the mutual attraction, and encouraged to proceed. Jaffe has cleverly set up the 8MinuteDating events so that people can indicate they are interested in meeting again for dating, business or friendship, but he tells singles if they really, really want to see someone again, they should check all three boxes just to maximize the odds.

For all the success these events have had, they still remain hampered by their limited scale, even in massive markets like New York City. When Crystal, a 40-year-old New York woman, recently tried to attend an 8MinuteDating event, she received a letter back from the company that she had been placed on the waiting list because more women than men had signed up. (Speed dating events for gays and lesbians don't have this problem.) The letter told Crystal she would be moved to the top of the list if she could enlist just one male friend or colleague to come along. It even offered hints on how to talk a guy into it. "Some men have expressed a fear of rejection at a dating event," the letter said. "One of the great aspects of 8MinuteDating is that there is no rejection. People comfortably talk without having to worry about asking someone out or being asked out." The company seemed to have overlooked one problem, though. If women were packing the room with all their platonic male friends, they would be less likely to meet a new love interest. "I mean, what was the point?" said Crystal. Speed dating may have some bugs to work out, but it has set off a new discussion about just how quick and efficient you can make the dating process. A *Los Angeles Times* reporter writing about the abundance of new dating options like speed dating observed that the trend seemed to be moving in the direction of ever-shorter encounters. "The next step," he joked, "is probably 'police lineup dating,' where single men and women are lined up like suspects and you identify which ones you'd like to date from behind a one-way windowless pane."

The move in the opposite direction, toward more thoughtful, time-consuming, low-tech, individualized meetings, may be just as compelling. Dating companies say that a good number of their customers show no interest in the new voice and video options, preferring the system as it has worked from the start, where you would have to imagine what a person was like from the written description. Similarly, some dating services have alienated users when they added more bells and whistles. One single man stopped using a dating site when it switched from showing him the number of people who had viewed his profile to revealing the online identities of all those people. All he could think was that every woman he had checked out, even momentarily, was going to be directed back to his picture, too, and he found it all a little too "Big Brotherish." Several of the happily married couples who met online a few years ago, moreover, say they are not certain they would date online again today. They were drawn to the intimate community that the

Internet once was, and are a little bit intimidated by what it has become today, a sprawling metropolis of diversity of all kinds.

Today, as more and more people opt to find dates from their home computers, or from cell phones while they are on the run, there seems to be insufficient evidence that the world is such an impersonal place that this is how you must find a mate unless you were lucky enough to snag one in college. Even Match.com found in a survey of its very own members that most people—office politics be damned—think it is fine to flirt at a company party. And, just in time for Valentine's Day 2003, the American Management Association reported that office romances were flourishing and were frowned upon less than ever, even when they involved a manager and a subordinate. About 45 percent of the managers who took part in that survey said that their office romance had led to marriage. The trend seemed to be growing, at least a little bit, with close to 70 percent of those managers in their thirties and forties saying they thought it was OK to date someone from the office, compared with 66 percent of managers in their fifties and sixties.

In her book *Not Just Friends*, Dr. Shirley Glass explores a new phenomenon of infidelity in which extramarital relationships are not forged on the Internet but develop gradually offline between men and women who share a close emotional friendship. Glass argues that such relationships are more common than ever, especially in the workplace, where men and women increasingly share equal professional status. "The traditional office relationship between men and women had the men in the power and the women in subordinate positions," said Glass. "Now, married men and women are forming very rich collegial relationships, working in an environment that is either very high pressured or very exciting." Although Glass' research focused on married people who inadvertently form relationships when they are not really looking, she agrees that the social intimacy bred in the workplace or other offline venues can make it a good place for single people to find love too. "Work is an ideal place to get to know someone without being part of the meat market," she said.

Recently, some high-priced matchmakers have admitted dipping into the online dating pool when they are really stumped trying to find a client a match. Now online dating companies have started considering how they might be less of a virtual meat market and more thoughtful matchmaker, at least for a segment of customers who prefer that approach. Some of these companies say they can conceive of, somewhere down the road, something like a "dating agent service," where you would pay a little extra to have a professional do most of the work. The most active online daters have sometimes sighed that keeping track of all their prospects feels like a job, so a "dating agent" service might attract busy professionals who have neither the time nor the interest in silly email exchanges that are going nowhere. Some dating company executives have even said privately that they would probably not use their own services as they function today, because the abundance of choices has become overwhelming and extremely time-consuming to wade through. Employing skilled agents to prescreen could also be a way of improving the odds that the people you meet online are of the caliber you seek.

There is always more work to be done on the psychological front as well, and although many dating sites say they do not wish to emulate the slow pace at which eHarmony.com operates, a number are adopting some of eHarmony's practices, offering their own version of a psychological profile to provide members one more way of narrowing down the field. While this approach is intriguing, some believe that psychology is unproven as a way for assessing matches and may ultimately be no more valuable than the entertainment it offers to a group of consumers who enjoy contemplating themselves. When Match.com employed its own psychologist to develop a way of profiling singles, it came up with a test that would match people based on their own character and the character type they were most likely to mesh with. Jeff Rudluff, vice president for new product development at Match.com, said he was interested, but not immediately sold. "My partner and I took the test, and it said we shouldn't be together," he said.

However, eHarmony is more confident than ever that a sound understanding of one's character is the best way to improve the odds of finding a lasting love connection. In some respects, the site's odds are already quite good. The company claims it produces five new marriages every single day. When it surveyed those married couples who met through its site, it concluded that their unions were exceptionally solid; eHarmony gave its couples the Dyadic Adjustment Scale test, a standard way of measuring the quality of a relationship, which asks couples questions like whether they have ever discussed divorce, stormed out of the house after a fight or regretted getting married. It said 62 percent of those who met through eHarmony and were married at least two years had above-average scores, compared with just 38 percent of those from the general population who had been married for the same length of time.

You'd think that would be enough for Dr. Warren, the company's founder and tireless innovator, to pass the baton. He's past the age that most people retire, and he has an established Web site that not only continues to attract new members, but also supports the sales of his multiple books and motivational tapes. Yet Warren remains frustrated. So much does he believe in the science behind the matching system he designed that he confesses he is perplexed that he isn't hearing about ten or more marriages every day. "It concerns me," he said. "While we are getting five new marriages a day, a lot of the matches we are making apparently are not working." As he sighed over his limited success, Warren started to chalk it all up to that mysterious chemistry factor. "I don't have the slightest idea how to match for chemistry," he conceded. "I mean I like women with small ankles. What does that mean? It is all just too complex."

But then he seemed to remember his mission, and said that his research was getting closer all the time to understanding chemistry, and taking all the mystery out of love. The future of matchmaking as Warren sees it, does not lie in advanced communicating technologies or accelerated dating schedules. His research to date has identified 29 dimensions ranging from intellect and curiosity to family background and "quality of self conception" on which couples ought to connect, and Warren is convinced there are many more equally important traits that have not yet been identified. "My dream is that some day this matching will be so precise that we will only have to give people three or four potential matches to choose from," he said. "I mean, I don't want to sound weird or anything, but a person's matching profile will be as complex as DNA or their blood type. We will get this matching down to a science."

13

SEX, COMPANIONSHIP AND THE USED-CAR DEALER

"To be successful requires taking risks, so here goes!"

—A 31-year-old Massachusetts woman

On a blustery afternoon in late January, Florence put on a lilac dress she selected because it was flattering but not too revealing. She drove to a local restaurant, and before the day was over, did something she had not done in well over 40 years. She held hands with a man. "My husband had never done that after we were married," she said, so she was pleased when Preston, her new Internet friend, took her hand as they went for a stroll after lunch. It was not what you would call an enchanted day. The restaurant where they had arranged to meet was closed, so they had to drive off in their separate cars to another place. Afterward, even if they had wanted nothing more than to walk off together into the sunset, it was too cold to stay outside for long. So Preston walked Florence back to her car, where

165

they stood and talked some more and prolonged their goodbye. He asked her what kind of movies she liked. He mentioned some other outings they might enjoy doing together. It was nice. Florence would like to have spent more time with him, but it seemed too forward to invite him back to her place right then, after they had just met. Too cozy inside. Too cold outside. So they agreed to talk some more another time, and as Florence went to get into her car, Preston leaned over and kissed her.

"On the lips," she said a few weeks later. "There weren't any sparks." But since Florence had not been especially interested in a sexual relationship, that had not bothered her. She and Preston had shared a close conversation, exchanging intimate details about their lives, some family troubles and some family tragedies. They had also laughed a lot. Their personalities had seemed to mesh. So Florence was surprised that three weeks after the date, she had not heard from him.

"My best guess," she said, "is that he met someone younger on the Internet."

For Florence, that disappointing conclusion to her first Internet encounter put an end to her online dating adventure. It seemed not to be worth the effort, all this emailing and calling and waiting to hear back. Not if it would end like this. It had been more than four months since Florence had registered for an online dating service, and she had been dutifully checking in every few days. She probably deserved an A for effort, but the project was pretty much a failure. The only men she had corresponded with at all were men she had contacted. After four months, she was still waiting for someone to initiate contact with her.

As Florence approached another Valentine's Day with no plans, Julie Fitzpatrick was growing hopeful. She was gradually learning more about Robert, the bushy-haired and balding 37-year-old computer consultant, who had been the only man she had found remotely interesting online. From his Internet profile, Fitzpatrick learned that Robert's best life skills were using humor to make friends laugh, managing his finances and remaining calm yet resilient during a crisis. Unlike so many of the other men on the eHarmony site, he had taken the time to consider who had been the most influential person in his life. He had offered a somewhat unusual response: the owner of a company he had worked for early in his career. "He was an honest and very smart person," Robert wrote. "He taught me a lot about relationships—business and personal." That fit in with the patience, the self-confidence and the industriousness that Julie Fitzpatrick had listed as the qualities she had to have in a mate. Even better, Robert said he had a sardonic sense of humor. Julie loved a sharp wit. After a few weeks of emailing, she was becoming more and more curious. She even said she felt "hungry" to meet him. One day he phoned her at the makeup counter where she worked. The call came in the middle of a "Get Your Smooch On" training session, about applying lipstick. "Have you got your smooch on?" she teased him.

For weeks, Annabel had given hardly a thought to her social life. Roger had never replied, even after her last note to reassure him that she did not look like a harried mom. Now, as the excitement of the New Year faded into the doldrums of midwinter in northern New England, the urge that had possessed her a few months earlier, the urge to have a man in her life, had passed. Annabel was back to being consumed with the usual demands of her life while striving to keep a positive attitude and not become overcome with bitterness toward her absentee ex. Sometimes she didn't know how he could live without his children. That would be impossible for her to bear. Yet sometimes when she woke up in the morning, all she could do was look forward to nine o'clock that night, when all three of the kids would be asleep. "I love them, but sometimes kids can be boring," she said.

And she still had not found a new car. The used-car dealer was slow. He'd take her on a test drive, have her all ready to buy one, and then at the last minute he would come back and say he had thought of another model she might like better. The whole cycle would start again: more research, more test drives...and more time with the used-car dealer. They were seeing each other at least once a week, talking on the phone a few times in between. She started to wonder if he was just stalling to have more time with her. It was not an unappealing idea. He was a father of three, divorced, and whenever Annabel ran into him around town, he seemed to have all his children in tow. She admired his family-man qualities. And of course, he knew a lot about cars.

Annabel's email box was as full as ever. New men continued to write, listing all kinds of qualities from a knack for fixing cars to a tendency to shop at Home Depot. But the novelty was gone. Annabel was not sure anymore if this was for her, if she had the stamina to converse with all of these men, let alone the nerve to meet a single one of them. So many people were doing it, but to her it still seemed unnatural. She also wondered if most of the men on the site weren't equally apprehensive, or just insincere. It was so easy to flirt when you had the computer as a buffer, but there were just too many questions that you couldn't answer over email. "You wonder, are a lot of these guys really afraid of meeting you?" she said. "Are they flirting with ten other women? Otherwise, why didn't they follow through?" She decided she would be more comfortable meeting someone offline, even if it took a little longer. She started thinking more about the family-man used-car dealer. He stayed in her thoughts even after she finally settled on a car and completed the purchase.

Then an idea came into her head. She had been thinking about driving to Florida with her children for spring break. She knew she would not be able to do all the driving alone, so she thought to suggest a combined road trip with the car guy and his three kids. "Is that like the kookiest thing?" she asked a friend. It was a little forward, she thought, but at the same time it made sense. They both had families to entertain, they could share the driving, and he was a used-car dealer; he could probably come up with some kind of vehicle big enough for the eight of them. It would be a good way to get to know him. She thought if he got over the initial shock of being invited away for a week with a very new acquaintance, he might see it the same way.

Nervously, she dialed the phone. He didn't sound so shocked by the invitation. He said he had been planning a different trip, to an amusement park in Pennsylvania. He invited Annabel and her family to join him there instead. After the winter they had been through, Annabel really wanted to go farther south. She pressed again for Florida. He said he would think about it. And as they got off the phone to get dinner for their respective families, they resolved to do one trip or the other when spring came.

Valentine's Day turned out just like every other day for Angelo DiMeglio. "Nothing special—would have liked it to have been," he said. "I bought myself some nice flowers and a box of candy. I went into town for an hour and it sucked. Not a lot of chicks out on Valentine's Day. It was kind of like going to the Boy Scout club."

DiMeglio was looking forward to the summer. "Hopefully I'll find love, sex and all that stuff, go to the beach, have a couple of friends and family visit, drink wine, take outdoor showers, maybe go away to Boston, Maine, New York, wherever," he said, one evening after the latest in a series of blizzards had left him stranded at home. "It's like it's never ending. But it's pretty around here when it snows."

Just having something to look forward to revived his spirits, and he resolved to lay low until the weather got warmer. The Internet had not brought a cure to his wintertime blues. "I'm up to 724 girls who viewed me," he said. "Pretty sickening that no one writes or responds."

Julie Fitzpatrick could not wait until Valentine's Day to see Robert. A few weeks earlier, on a Wednesday evening, she dressed up in a casual but sexy black lace-up top and went to meet him at his favorite steakhouse. The room was crowded, and she became fearful that she would not be able to find him, but right away, a 5'8" guy with bushy hair and a receding hairline whom she recognized from the photo approached. She breathed a sigh of relief. She had always been drawn to men with just his kind of looks. "He had a soft face and nice features," she said. "Right away I thought he was absolutely adorable, and beautiful."

There was the briefest moment of awkwardness, when they looked around the room and worried that it would take a long time to get a table, but within minutes a table at the bar became available, a table that Robert remarked was in the perfect location for some people-watching. "Something I love to do too," Fitzpatrick gushed the next day when she had settled down enough to review all that she had in common with this man she had met in the most improbable place, online. "I immediately felt at ease."

Five minutes after they got their table at the bar, Robert did something that made Julie feel even more at ease. "He pulled a pack of cigarettes out of his pocket and set them down," she said. "I thought, 'Oh good, he smokes too.'"

Between cigarettes, they shared two appetizers, ordered salads and mulled over the main course menu. Julie loved food, but she preferred grazing all day to sitting down at a big meal. And, in keeping with the harmonious tone that had quickly been set for the evening, Robert told her he was exactly the same way. They decided to forget the entrée and have a couple more drinks instead. They chatted incessantly, just like the computer had said they would. They stayed until the restaurant was closing, not even looking up long enough to know that it was closing. Someone had to tell them. "Who noticed?" said Fitzpatrick. "We were so into each other."

The next morning she checked her email and found a note from Robert. He had written to say he could not wait to see her again.

Thanks to online dating, Julie Fitzpatrick had her happiest Valentine's Day in years. Reuters.

Was this normal, for her to react this way to a man she had just met? "On a blind date?" she replied. "Never, ever, ever. This date with Robert was out of this world," she said, beaming. "We are so into each other. It was instant attraction, total chemistry."

The following week, after a few more dinners of incessant conversation and gazing into each other's eyes, Robert asked Julie if she would be his Valentine. On a freezing cold Valentine's Day they went out for a nice dinner. It had been only two weeks, but she felt like she had known him forever. Things went a little less smoothly that night. On the drive home, Robert was stopped by the police and given the Breathalyzer test. He wasn't drunk though, maybe just a little drunk with love. The police let him continue on his way, but Robert said he had half wanted to be ordered to pull over to the side of the road for a while so that he and Julie could cuddle in the car.

"I have not been in a relationship in five years, and I cannot imagine a better match," she said when they passed the one-month mark, still stunned by her good fortune. She knew other issues would come up as the relationship progressed. They always did. For the moment, though, things were going so well that she said she could not imagine what those issues would be. She didn't need makeup anymore to produce that happy glow, and as she arrived at work each morning brimming with joy, several of the other makeup artists in the store asked her to tell them more about how she had found such a nice man.

INDEX

A

Abu-Ghazaleh, Talal, 86
Adams, John, 96–97
Affiliate Goddess, 48
Affiliate marketing
     programs, 47–48
Alejandro, Delis, 120
Amazon.com, 36
America Online, ICQ online
     community, 93–94
Andrew, 52
Angermann, Melanie, 12–13,
     137–138, 142–144

Annabel, 1–3, 64, 103–105,
     109, 110, 167–169
Anonymity of online
     environment, 122
Arab Marriage
     Connection, 59
Arab2Love.com, 81
Attraction vs. compatibility,
     60–61

B

Background checks, 43
Bailey, Beth, 15